WALLPAPER
TAPETEN
PAPIERS PEINTS

TAPETEN | PAPIERS PEINTS

WALLPAPER

JOACHIM FISCHER

h.f.ullmann

Contents | Inhaltsverzeichnis | Sommaire

Introduction

The architectural revolution of the 1920s precipitated the transformation of traditional, figured wallpaper into a medium for color and little else. As Le Corbusier proclaimed in 1925: "Aimer la pureté!" (Love the pure!). Yet leaving the walls of his "machines for living" entirely bare was too purist even for this acknowledged enemy of anything decorative. Although he defined it as "painting by machine," Le Corbusier went on to design his own collection of monochrome wallpaper. A little earlier, the Weimar Bauhaus group had launched the minimalist Bauhaus Wallpaper line, distinguished by innovative textural effects. The decline of ornament in favor of color made the predominance of ingrain (wood-chip) wallpaper possible. The high and low ends of the market drifted further and further apart, with the cheaper mass produced varieties gradually replacing innovative design. Then designers like Ulf Moritz, Andrea Pössnicker, Karim Rashid and many others made wallpaper innovative once again. Their collections of the past few years have worked with new techniques including unusual optical effects and block printing. The current trend toward expressive wallpaper and individualized wall decor suggests that the pendulum may be moving once again in the direction of pattern and design.

Wallpaper is experiencing a comeback, freed from its sad fate as a lifeless, unimaginative, plain and often aesthetically questionable wall covering. Clients can now have individualized wall treatments made to order. Wallpaper is no longer merely a modest attempt to cover-up bare spots, but haute couture for walls. Artistic quality presupposes meticulous execution of the design so that each and every motif can be distinguished, precisely, down to the last detail. The dyes for individual wallpapers are mixed by hand, taking into account every nuance of color, and then applied using different paint and patina techniques, including screen painting. The pattern spectrum is categorically broad, ranging from bold, modern graphic elements to delicate ornamentation. Details and limited edition series that were once an expensive luxury, and which were not made for a long time for technical reasons, are possible again today thanks to computer assisted production processes. The mistrust generated by decorated surfaces has given way to a celebration of opulence. Contemporary architects who work with pattern find themselves in a paradoxical situation. In seeking clear and rational forms, they are following the precepts of modernism—but these premises are now challenged by the long suppressed resurgence of surface decoration.

Erste Anfänge des Trends, den traditionell bildlichen Charakter des papiernen Wandschmucks in Farbe aufzulösen, sind mit der Architekturwende der zwanziger Jahre verknüpft. „Aimer la pureté!", propagierte 1925 Le Corbusier. Doch die Wände seiner Wohnmaschinen ganz unverkleidet zu belassen, erschien dem „Dekorstürmer" dann doch zu puristisch. Er definierte die Tapete in „peinture à la machine" um und entwarf eine Kollektion unifarbener Tapeten. Kurz zuvor hatten die Weimarer Gestalter ihre minimalistischen „Bauhaus-Tapeten" mit neuartigen Rauharz-Effekten lanciert. Die Auflösung des Ornaments in Farbe ermöglichte den Siegeszug der Raufasertapete. High und Low End des Angebotsspektrums drifteten bald auseinander und das Geschäft mit billiger Massenware verdrängte allmählich das innovative Design. Neues aufs Tapet brachten dann Designer wie Ulf Moritz, Andrea Pößnicker, Karim Rashid und andere. Deren Kollektionen der letzten Jahre setzen auf effektvolle Oberflächenoptik und auf Handdrucktapeten. Dass das Pendel sogar wieder in Richtung Muster ausschlagen kann, beweist der aktuelle Trend zur ausdrucksstarken Tapete und individuellen Wandgestaltung.

Die Tapete erlebt ihr Comeback und wird aus der Tristesse, der lieb- und einfallslosen Rolle als schlichte und oftmals ästhetisch zweifelhafte Wandbedeckung, befreit. Für jeden Kunden werden maßgeschneiderte Wandgestaltungen erschaffen – Haute Couture für Wände statt schamhafte Bedeckung der Blöße. Künstlerische Qualität erfordert Genauigkeit am Objekt und da sich die Objekte unterscheiden braucht es Vielfalt, auch und gerade im Detail. Um auch geringste Nuancen bei der Farbgebung zu berücksichtigen, werden die Farben für jede Tapete individuell gemischt und mit unterschiedlichen Mal- und Patiniertechniken oder im Siebdruckverfahren aufgetragen. Das Spektrum an Mustern ist breit gefächert: von klaren, modernen und graphischen Elementen bis hin zu verspielten Ornamenten. Details und Kleinstserien die bisher einen teuren Luxus darstellten und lange Zeit technisch nicht darstellbar waren, werden heute durch computergestützte Produktionsverfahren ermöglicht. Das Misstrauen gegenüber den geschmückten Oberflächen weicht nun einer Freude an opulenter Ornamentik. Zeitgenössische Architekten, die mit Mustern arbeiten, befinden sich in einer paradoxen Situation. Zwar folgen sie den Forderungen der Moderne nach einer rationalen Gestaltung, dennoch verhelfen sie der lange verdrängten Dekoration der Oberflächen zu einem Durchbruch.

Les débuts de la tendance à remplacer la tapisserie décorative tradition-
nelle par de la peinture sont liés à l'évolution de l'architecture dans les
années 1920. En 1925, Le Corbusier propageait : « Aimez la pureté ! » Toutefois, le pionnier de l'architecture ne voulait pas forcer sur le purisme
en laissant sans aucun revêtement les murs de ses «machines à habiter ».
Aussi redéfinit-il la tapisserie en « peinture à la machine » en créant une
collection de papiers peints unis. Peu de temps auparavant, les designers
de Weimar avaient lancé leurs papiers peints Bauhaus minimalistes,
dont l'apparence rugueuse était alors inédite. Le remplacement du motif
ornemental au profit de la couleur annonça la conquête du papier blanc
à peindre. Il y eut bientôt un bas et un haut de gamme, avec d'énormes
différences de qualités, la décoration avec des produits de masse bon marché évinçant peu à peu le design avant-gardiste. Des designers tels que
Ulf Moritz, Andrea Pößnicker, Karim Rashid, et bien d'autres encore, ont
fait souffler un vent nouveau sur la tapisserie. Leurs récentes collections
misent sur des papiers peints réalisés à la main et sur les effets visuels
obtenus par le revêtement mural. Les tendances s'orientent à nouveau
vers les motifs, ainsi qu'en témoignent la vogue actuelle de papiers peints
ornementaux et la décoration personnalisée des murs.

La tapisserie fait un retour triomphal ; elle n'a plus rien de commun avec
les simples rouleaux de papiers peints, de facture plus ou moins esthétique, dont le rôle se bornait à tapisser les murs. Aujourd'hui, la décoration
murale est individualisée selon les goûts et les besoins des clients – de la
haute couture pour les murs au lieu de la nécessité d'habiller des surfaces
nues. La qualité artistique exige une grande précision, de même qu'une
grande diversité de méthodes dans le cadre de l'élaboration de pièces ori-
ginales. Le détail est notamment important : pour chaque papier peint,
les couleurs sont mélangées individuellement jusqu'à l'obtention de la
nuance recherchée, puis appliquées à l'aide de diverses techniques de
peinture, de patine ou encore de sérigraphie. Le large éventail de motifs
s'étend des figures modernes aux lignes graphiques nettes jusqu'aux ornements extravagants. Aujourd'hui, grâce à l'ordinateur, on a accès à des
méthodes permettant de fabriquer des articles qui n'étaient pas réalisa-
bles techniquement ou étaient produits en petites quantités de manière
très onéreuse. La méfiance envers la tapisserie surchargée d'antan s'est
effacée devant l'envie d'une ornementation opulente. Les architectes
d'intérieurs contemporains se retrouvent dans une situation paradoxale.
Ils suivent certes les exigences modernes d'aménagement rationnel, tout
en soutenant le renouveau d'un désir longuement refoulé de décoration
murale exubérante.

Kreationen | Créations

Creations

Design Object Wallpapers

This design group is always on the lookout for a familiar motif to transform into something imaginative, playful and new. 5.5 Designer's inventiveness and work methods have received widespread acclaim. While searching for new means of expression, they discovered wallpaper itself. Their designs based on humorous variations on the theme of "wallpaper patterns" are particularly effective. Their work consists of hand painted or block printed pieces of wallpaper complemented by the appropriate accessories, projecting a strong, three-dimensional quality. The designs of 5.5 Designers walk the fine line between art for art's sake, ironic provocation and pleasing decoration.

Tapetenobjekte

Die Designgruppe ist immer wieder auf der Suche nach altbekanntem und kombinieren dieses mit ideenreichem und spielerisch Neuem. Ihr Ideenreichtum und ihre Arbeitsweise wurden bis heute regelmäßig ausgezeichnet. Auf der Suche nach neuen Ausdrucksmitteln haben Sie auch die Tapete für sich entdeckt. Ihre Entwürfe überzeugen durch den humorvollen Umgang mit dem Thema „Tapetenmuster". Diese Muster, handgemalte oder ausgedruckte Tapetenfragmente, werden mit entsprechenden Accessoires ergänzt und somit überwiegend dreidimensional dargestellt. Die Entwürfe von 5.5 Designers sind eine Gradwanderung zwischen künstlerischem Selbstzweck, ironischer Provokation und gefälliger Dekoration.

Éléments décoratifs

Ces designers ne cessent de rechercher des formes traditionnelles qu'ils associent à une foison d'innovations ludiques. Leur richesse d'idées et leur mode de travail leur ont déjà valu de nombreux prix. À la recherche de nouveaux moyens d'expression, ils ont redécouvert le papier peint. Pleines d'humour, leurs réalisations sur le thème « motifs de tapisserie » ont tout pour charmer le regard. Fragments peints à la main ou imprimés, leurs motifs sont pour la plupart complétés par des accessoires choisis, afin de former un décor tridimensionnel. Les créations de 5.5 Designers jouent sur trois facettes : elles sont œuvres d'art, provocation ironique et décoration harmonieuse.

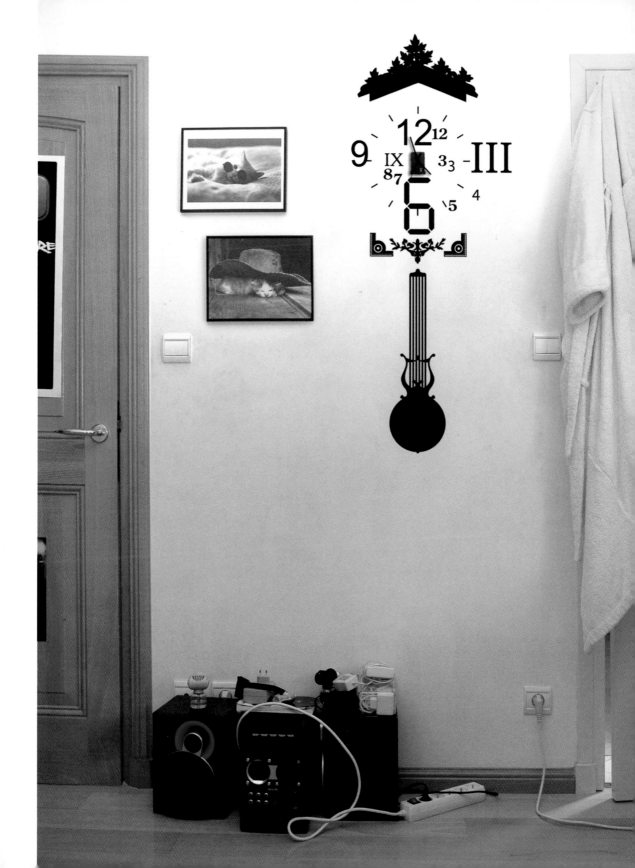

This wall treatment combines three-dimensionality with emotional and material complexity. The walls are not mere bearers of graphic design, but elements that define space and atmosphere.

Diese Variante der Wandgestaltung vereint Dreidimensionalität mit einer Gefühls- und Material-vielfalt. Sie sind nicht nur Träger grafischer Elemente, sondern bestimmen den Raum und seine Atmosphäre.

Cette forme d'aménagement mural réunit le tridimensionnel à une riche diversité d'idées fantaisistes et de matériaux. Dépassant leur rôle de compositions graphiques, les éléments décoratifs caractérisent la pièce et son ambiance.

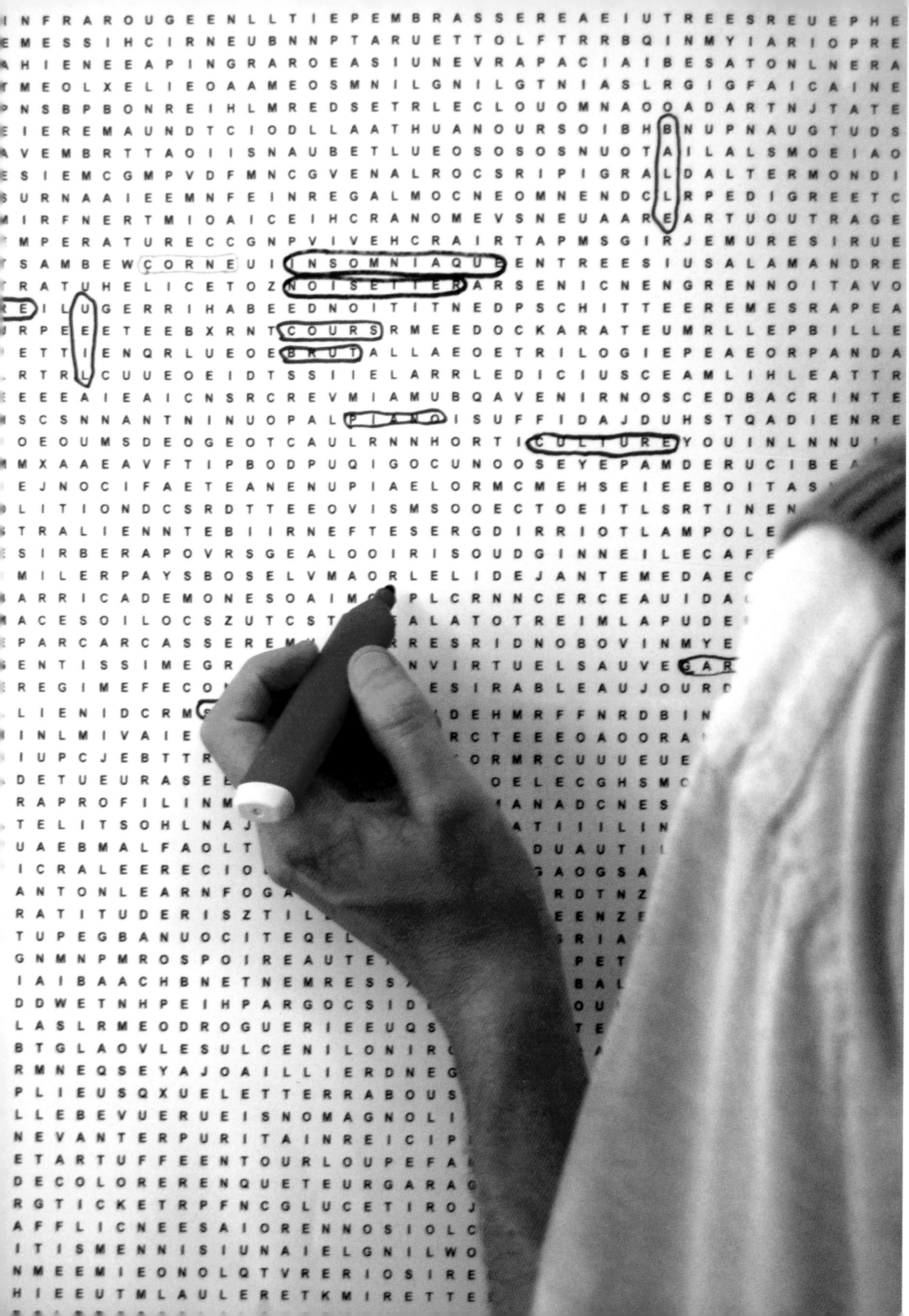

This wallpaper is stamped with letters like a giant word search puzzle. Colored markers are provided to group the letters into words. In this way, the room is constantly changing.

Die Tapete ist gleichmäßig mit Buchstaben bedruckt. Mit farbigen Stiften können die Buchstaben zu Worten verbunden werden. Dadurch verändert sich der Raum ständig.

La tapisserie est imprimée de rangées régulières de lettres dont on fait des mots en les reliant à l'aide de marqueurs de diverses couleurs. On peut ainsi changer le décor à volonté.

After this wallpaper is pasted to the wall, the pattern can be filled in with markers, giving each room its own individual decorative note.

Klebt die Tapete an der Wand, können mit Stiften die Muster ausgemalt werden. Somit wird dem Raum eine individuelle Note verliehen.

Une fois le papier peint collé au mur, on peut laisser libre cours à sa fantaisie en créant des motifs avec des marqueurs, ce qui donne une touche individuelle à la pièce.

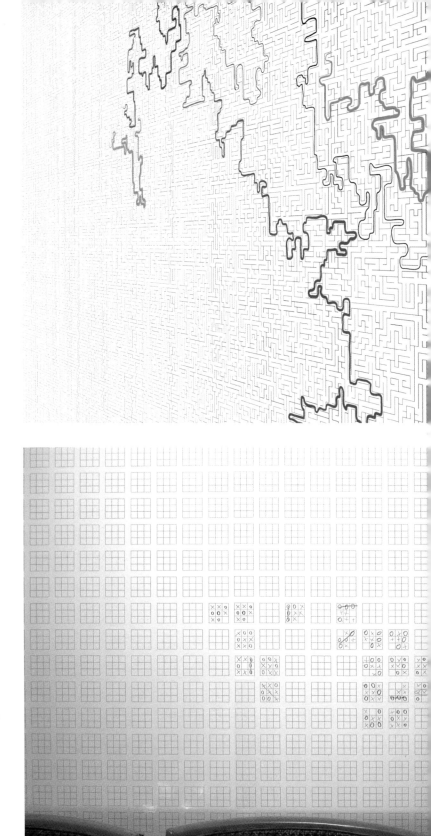

Wallstickers

"A better tomorrow" is an international meeting place and clearing house for unusual, eccentric design far removed from mass production. Anyone looking for that distinctive, unmistakable something is in the right place here. It is a place where anyone can come in, submit a design, and offer it for sale. Every manner of fashion accessory and decorative art is available, from handbags, belts and prints to furniture. A better tomorrow is a forum that offers young designers with fresh, untried ideas the opportunity to test their products on the open market. Imagination is the only requirement. Wallstickers can be used to brighten up walls, floors or even furniture. Combining different wallstickers with one another leads to endless possibilities and variations. Gently detach the sticker from its template, stick it on the wall, and enjoy!

Wallsticker

Das Label „A better tomorrow" ist Anlaufstelle für ausgefallenes Design, abseits von Massenversendern. Wer das gewisse, das unverwechselbare Etwas sucht ist hier richtig. Hier kann jeder seine Motive hochladen und anbieten. Von Accessoires, Taschen, Gürteln, Prints bis hin zu Möbeln sind Labels aller Art vertreten. Vor allem für junge Designer mit frischen, unverbrauchten Ideen bietet diese Plattform eine Chance, sich und seine Produkte auszuprobieren. Dabei ist Phantasie alles, was gefragt ist. Mit den Wallstickern hat man die Möglichkeit Boden, Wände, ja sogar Möbel zu verschönern. Zudem kann man alle Wallsticker untereinander kombinieren, dies verschafft unendliche Möglichkeiten und Varianten. Einfach mit ein bisschen Fingerspitzengefühl die Sticker vom Trägermaterial lösen, an die Wand kleben und sich freuen.

Stickers décoratifs

Le label « A better tomorrow » est un site Internet qui accueille tout ce qu'il y a d'extravagant dans le design, à des années-lumière de la distribution de masse. Quiconque recherche l'objet unique, le « quelque chose en plus » trouvera ici son bonheur. Chacun peut y présenter et proposer ses créations. Des accessoires aux sacs, ceintures, gravures et meubles, a better tomorrow réunit un grand nombre de designers. Ce site offre notamment aux jeunes créateurs débordant d'idées nouvelles la chance d'exposer leurs produits et de se faire un nom. Le seul critère exigé est la fantaisie. La vaste gamme des stickers décoratifs permet d'embellir les murs, les sols et même les meubles. On peut par ailleurs les combiner et créer une multitude de décors différents. Il suffit d'un peu de doigté pour détacher les motifs adhésifs de leurs supports et les coller au mur, avant de s'enthousiasmer à la vue des résultats.

It seems like these small green men have already occupied the room and are getting ready to surprise the visitor.

Die kleinen grünen Männchen scheinen diesen Raum bereits eingenommen zu haben und werden den Besucher in Erstaunen versetzen.

Des petites créatures vertes ont pris possession de cette pièce ; leur présence plonge le visiteur dans l'étonnement.

The exceptional graphics held in clear and luminescent colors have their distinctive language.

Die ungewöhnlichen Grafiken in kräftigen und leuchtenden Farben haben ihre ganz eigene Sprache.

Des dessins insolites réalisés dans des couleurs vives ont un langage qui leur est propre.

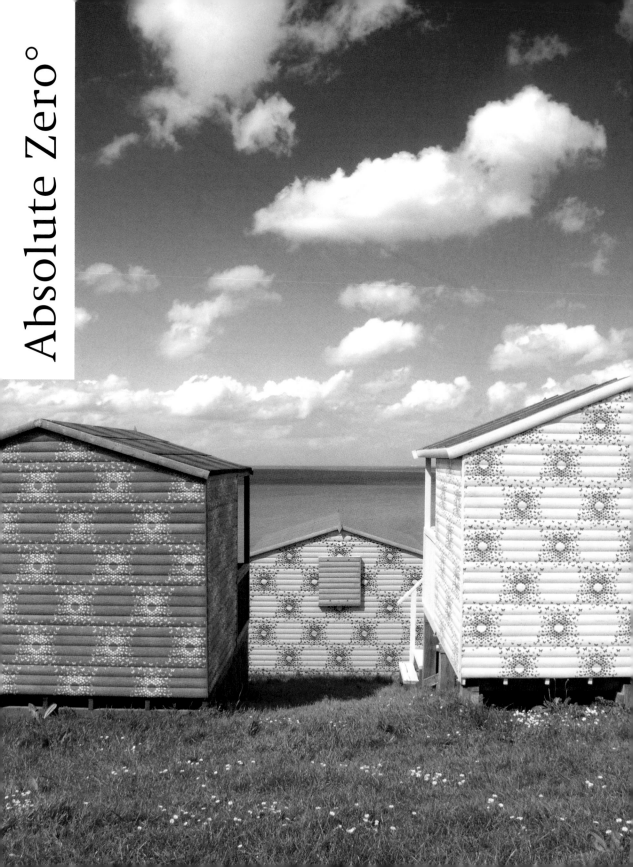

Absolute Zero°

Design Object Wallpapers

The wallpaper collections of this London agency are comical and appealing. The inspiration for the Playtime product line came from a number of sources. The somewhat nostalgic name comes from playtime crackers, which are children's party toys with small treats inside. The richly decorated textiles of Giraud for Herman Miller were stylistic influences. The names and inspiration behind the individual designs are also unusual. A photograph showing different house numbers led to Knock-Knock, the most popular design in the Playtime line. Seemingly screwed into the wall, in Knock-Knock numbers are understood as significant elements in daily life, an indication that mathematics doesn't have to be abstract.

Tapetenobjekte

Die Tapetenkollektion der Londoner Agentur wurde gestaltet, um ansprechende und skurrile Tapeten anzubieten. Inspirationen für die Produktpalette Playtime stammen aus verschiedenen Quellen. Der etwas nostalgische Name ist der einer Kekssorte, deren Plätzchenformen einfacher Spielsachen oder Tiere entsprachen. Einfluss auf das Design nahmen auch die reich verzierten Textilien von Giraud für Herman Miller. Auch die Bezeichnungen und Einflüsse für die verschiedenen Produkte sind ungewöhnlich: Die beliebteste Tapete „Knock-Knock", entstand nach dem Fotografieren verschiedener Hausnummern. Zahlen, die angeschraubt zu sein scheinen, zeigen ihre Bedeutung im täglichen Leben, und dass Mathematik nicht abstrakt sein muss.

Panneaux décoratifs

Créer une collection de papiers peints se distinguant par sa singularité était l'objectif de la firme londonienne Absolute Zero Degrees. Diverses sources ont inspiré la gamme des produits *Playtime*. Ce nom à l'accent nostalgique est celui d'une marque de biscuits dont les formes élémentaires représentaient des jouets ou des animaux. Les textiles richement ornés de Giraud créés pour Hermann Miller ont également influencé le design. En fait, les appellations et les sources d'inspiration à l'origine des papiers peints sont toutes particulières : par exemple, la tapisserie très populaire *Knock-Knock* a été créée à partir de photographies de numéros de maisons. Ces chiffres qui semblent cloués sur le mur ont une grande importance dans la vie quotidienne ; les mathématiques ne sont pas toujours abstraites.

Wallpaper doesn't only cover interior walls, but also the exterior.

Tapeten überziehen nicht nur Innenwände sondern auch Außenwände.

Le papier peint ne tapisse pas seulement les parois intérieures, mais aussi les murs extérieurs.

What started out as experimental is today a popular wallpaper pattern.

Was als Experiment begann, ist heute ein angesagtes Tapetenmuster.

Expérimentation au départ, ce papier peint est aujourd'hui très tendance.

This wallpaper was named Battery Square after a street in Portmeiron, Wales where the cult television series The Prisoner was filmed. The design represents a surrealistic arrangement of the village with towers, domes and a unicorn.

„Battery Square" – benannt nach der englischen Kult-Serie The Prisoner – zeigt eine surrealistische Abbildung des Dorfes mit seinen Türmen, Kuppeln und einem Einhorn.

Battery Square – papier peint nommé d'après la série anglaise culte *Le Prisonnier* – montre une image surréaliste du village avec ses tours, ses coupoles et une licorne.

The wallpaper called Do You Live in A Town is an imaginative representation of city life and living.

Die Tapete, mit dem Namen „Do You Live In A Town", zeigt auf phantasievolle Weise städtisches Wohnen und Leben.

La tapisserie appelée *Do You live In a Town* figure avec fantaisie la vie et l'habitat citadins.

Bruno Munari's

ABC

Semplice lezione di inglese

Birgit Amadori

Hotel Fox

The magical illustrations of the German illustrator Birgit Amadori are influenced by legends, myths, and fairytales from a wide range of different civilizations. In her unique way, the artist combines western and oriental pictorial motives in her pictures. Colors and patterns result in an imaginative unity, as can be seen in her creations of the three hotel rooms and the mural painting on the landing. For the room named King's Forest, she created a magic forest in which a fox guides a figure through the mythical forest world.

Hotel Fox

Die märchenhaften Tapeten der Illustratorin Birgit Amadori sind von Sagen, Mythen und Legenden aus den verschiedensten Kulturkreisen beeinflusst. In ihren Bildern kombiniert die Künstlerin auf unnachahmliche Weise westliche und orientalische Bildmotive miteinander. Farben und Muster ergeben eine phantasievolle Einheit. Das ist auch in den drei Zimmer und dem Wandbild am Treppenabsatz, die von ihr gestaltet wurden, zu sehen. Für das Zimmer King's Forest entstand ein Zauberwald, in dem der Fuchs (Fox) eine Gestalt durch die mystische Welt des Waldes geleiten soll.

Hôtel Fox

Contes, légendes et mythes de tous les pays ont inspiré les papiers peints féeriques de l'illustratrice Birgit Amadori. Unique en son genre, l'artiste associe dans ses illustrations des motifs de facture occidentale et orientale, dont les couleurs et les lignes forment des ensembles d'une exquise originalité. On découvre ses magnifiques créations dans les trois chambres et dans la décoration murale de la cage d'escalier qu'elle a signées. La chambre King's Forest est ornée d'une forêt enchantée dans laquelle le renard (fox) guide un personnage à travers le monde mythique de la forêt.

In contrast, Amadori chose a cool, restrained blue as the base color for her King's Court 1 and 2 rooms, representing the royal virtues of faith, loyalty and honor. Blue is the color of the sky and sea, symbolizing endless freedom. The figures include the king and his consort, their magicians, fools, and soothsayers.

Für die beiden King's Court Zimmer wählte die Grafikerin dagegen kühles und zurückhaltendes Blau als Grundfarbe. Es verweist auf königliche Tugenden wie Glaube, Treue und Ehre. Und es ist die Farbe des Himmels und des Meeres und symbolisiert damit unendliche Freiheit. Hier versammeln sich auf den Tapeten der König und seine Gemahlin mit ihren Magiern, Hofnarren und Wahrsagern.

Dans les deux chambres King's Court, la créatrice a choisi comme coloris de base des bleus froids et sobres. Le bleu évoque des vertus royales telles que la foi, la fidélité et l'honneur. Également couleur du ciel et de la mer, il symbolise la liberté infinie. Sur la tapisserie sont réunis le roi, la reine et ses magiciens, les fous de la cour et les devins.

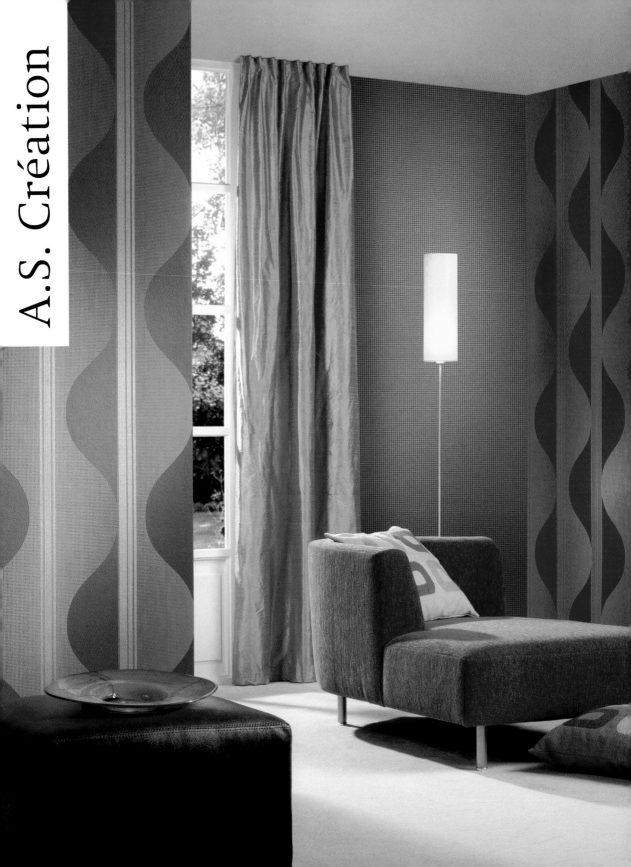

A.S. Création

Retro DeLuxe

Varied combinations of horizontal and vertical elements in every possible combination of colors contribute to these creative wall treatments well off the beaten track of form and design. The formal variations are almost inexhaustible. The designs are the product of A.S. Création, Europe's leading wallpaper manufacturer. They are marketed under the name Fascination, the brand for wallpaper meeting the highest standard of interior design. A.S. Création is also the founder of a wallpaper foundation of the same name, and is also the force behind the wallpaper design competition "New Walls, Please!" Among its many functions, the publicly accessible A.S. Création Wallpaper Foundation conducts research on the cultural aspects of wallpaper, funds further development and supports education programs for wallpaper design.

Retro DeLuxe

Waagerechte und senkrechte Kombinationen, in allen Varianten und Farbkompositionen, ermöglichen Wandkreationen jenseits ausgetretener Gestaltungspfade. Die Gestaltungsvarianten sind nahezu unerschöpflich. Die Firma A.S. Création ist Europas führender Hersteller von Tapeten. Das Unternehmen prägte den Begriff „Faszination Tapete" – Tapetenkollektion für höchste Ansprüche im Interieur-Bereich. Weiterhin ist A.S. Création Gründer der gleichnamigen Tapetenstiftung und Erfinder des Tapetenwettbewerbes „New Walls, Please!". Seit ihrer Gründung verfolgt die gemeinnützige A.S. Création Tapetenstiftung unter anderem das Ziel, die kulturellen Aspekte der Tapete zu erforschen, ihre Weiterentwicklung zu fördern und die Ausbildung im Tapetendesign zu unterstützen.

Retro DeLuxe

Des compositions verticales et horizontales, aux multiples variations de motifs et de couleurs, offrent des créations murales à l'écart des sentiers battus. La foison de possibilités décoratives est pratiquement inépuisable. La société A.S. Création est le leader européen du papier peint. Ce fabricant allemand, dont le mot d'ordre est : « fascination du papier peint », propose des articles de très haute gamme pour les espaces intérieurs. A.S. Création a en outre créé la fondation de tapisserie éponyme et initié le concours « New Walls, Please! » (de nouveaux murs, S.V.P. !). Depuis ses débuts, cette fondation d'intérêt général a entre autres pour objectif l'étude des aspects culturels de la tapisserie et encourage son développement ainsi que la formation de créateurs dans ce domaine.

Wallpaper creates a mood, giving the home its own individual ambience.

Mit Tapeten lassen sich sinnliche Stimmungen kreieren, die das eigene Zuhause zu einem individuellen Wohlfühl-Ambiente machen.

La tapisserie est un moyen de créer une atmosphère personnalisée qui confère une ambiance de bien-être, sensuelle ou douillette, à son lieu de vie.

Wallpaper can look as if it has been hand-painted by an artist with a fine-tipped brush.

Tapeten sehen aus, als ob sie in künstlerischer Handarbeit mit feinem Pinsel gemalt seien.

On pourrait croire qu'une main d'artiste a décoré ces papiers au pinceau fin.

Everything is in flux. Wallpaper can be decorated with delicate patterns or bold, oversized ornamentation.

Alles ist im Fluss. Tapeten als Kleinmuster oder in großformatigen Ornamenten.

Tout est permis dans une décoration réussie. Des papiers peints aux petits motifs ou ornés de dessins grand format.

One individual's idea can be the spark that sets off a new trend.

Die Idee eines Einzelnen kann der Funke sein, der einen neuen Trend entfacht.

L'idée brillante d'un créateur peut être à l'origine d'une nouvelle tendance.

Dessoustapete

Sandra Hagedorn and Olivier Arcioli, designers and founders of AtelierGrün, wanted to build a bridge between printed and spatial media. According to their conception, wallpaper should surrender its purely decorative aesthetic and ornamental function and become more of a medium for expression. Living in a room should broaden and alter its meaning. Their multi-layered wallpaper provides the opportunity to experience the real space as part of an ever-changing reality. The initial visual impression is of a run of the mill, baroque, ornament-patterned wall. But when the visitor looks at the same wallpaper through a filter of red plastic film, a hidden, content-rich world comes into view.

Dessoustapete

Sandra Hagedorn und Olivier Arcioli, Designer und Gründer von AtelierGrün, wollen eine Brücke zwischen gedruckten und räumlichen Medien schaffen. Ihrer Auffassung nach soll die Tapete ihren, in der Regel, rein dekorativen und ästhetischen Charakter als Ornament verlieren und vielmehr zu einem Ausdrucksmedium werden, dass das Leben im Raum erweitert und verändert. Der Betrachter hat die Möglichkeit, über diese vielschichtige Tapete, den realen Raum als veränderte Wirklichkeit zu erleben. Vom visuellen Eindruck wirkt die Tapete im ersten Moment wie eine ganz normale, barocke und ornamentale Musterwand. Doch wenn der Betrachter dieselbe Tapete durch die rote Folie betrachtet, taucht eine versteckte, inhaltliche Ebene auf.

Dessoustapete

Sandra Hagedorn et Olivier Arcioli, designers et fondateurs d'AtelierGrün, se sont donné pour objectif d'associer les notions d'espace et d'imprimés. Selon eux, le papier peint devrait perdre son caractère purement décoratif et esthétique qui n'en fait qu'un ornement, pour devenir un médium expressif destiné à modifier et élargir un espace. L'observateur perçoit la pièce dans une réalité modifiée à travers ces papiers peints complexes. Au premier regard, la tapisserie ne se distingue aucunement d'un papier peint habituel de style baroque, au décor ornemental. Mais en regardant à travers le film de couleur rouge, on découvre une autre face et son contenu caché.

The Dessous Wallpaper project represents an attempt to analyze what are normally considered the boundaries of a space and define them anew. Are the walls with their wallpaper the true borders of a space, or is space an abstraction without boundaries?

Bei dem Projekt Dessoustapete handelt es sich um den Versuch, den gewöhnlich als Begrenzung verstandenen Begriff des Raumes zu hinterfragen und neu zu definieren. Sind die Wände mit ihren Tapeten die Grenzen von Raum oder ist Raum etwas grenzenloses und abstraktes?

Le projet *Dessoustapete* cherche à remettre en question la notion habituelle de limite de l'espace, pour tenter ensuite de la redéfinir. Est-ce que les murs tapissés délimitent l'espace ou l'espace est-il infini et abstrait ?

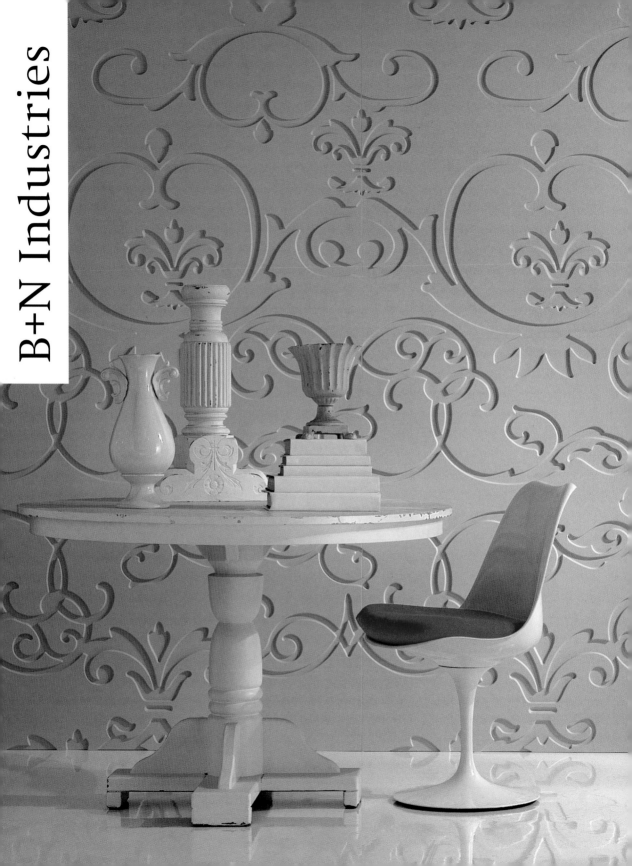

Iconic

B+N Industries is an innovative design and manufacturing company that sells its products to retail stores, the consumer goods industry and architecture firms. Its designers are always providing a fresh perspective, offering new solutions to the ever-changing market for interior design. The production of their relief-decorated wall coverings involves the innovative process of applying layers of laminate over a carved wooden core. The unbelievably durable result can be sawed into panels, nailed, screwed, glued or simply hung on the wall.

Iconic

B+N Industries ist ein innovatives Design- und Fertigungsunternehmen mit Produkten und Systemen für den Einzelhandel, die Konsumgüterindustrie und die Architektur. Hierfür entwickeln die Gestalter überraschend neue, funktionale Lösungen zur Aufwertung des Lebensraumes. B+N bringt regelmäßig neue Lösungen auf einen sich ständig ändernden Markt der Innenraumgestaltung und eröffnet dadurch der Designbranche frische Perspektiven. Zur Herstellung der reliefverzierten Wandverkleidungen werden in einem innovativen Verfahren Laminatschichten über einen geschnitzten Holzkern gezogen. Mit ihrer unglaublich langlebigen Beschaffenheit kann man die Paneele zersägen, vernageln, verschrauben, verkleben oder einfach nur so an die Wand hängen.

Iconic

B+N Industries est le nom d'une société innovatrice de design et de fabrication proposant des produits et des systèmes destinés au commerce, à l'industrie de biens de consommation et aux architectes. Les créateurs développent des solutions surprenantes, inédites et fonctionnelles destinées à valoriser les pièces à vivre. B+N Industries apporte régulièrement des solutions sur un marché de l'architecture d'intérieur sans cesse en évolution, ouvrant ainsi de nouvelles perspectives au secteur du design. Dans la fabrication des revêtements muraux en relief, un procédé innovant est utilisé : des couches de laminat épousent un support en bois sculpté. Aussi résistants qu'endurants, les panneaux peuvent être sciés, fixés avec des pointes ou des clous, collés ou tout simplement accrochés aux murs.

Matte and glossy surfaces create an exciting play of light and reflection.

Durch die Verbindung matter und glänzender Oberflächen entsteht ein spannendes Spiel mit Licht und Reflektionen.

Les surfaces mates et brillantes produisent des effets de lumière et des reflets fascinants.

Bold patterns executed in high gloss lacquer are made more vivid by the extreme matte background.

Kraftvolle Muster in glänzendem Lack korrespondieren optimal mit dem extrem matten Fond.

Les motifs laqués aux lignes vigoureuses s'accordent parfaitement avec le fond mat.

bernjus.gisbertz atelier

25hours Hotel

Contemporary design, individual style and good service for a moderate price—these are qualities that describe the 25hours Hotel very well indeed. The 95 rooms and seven suites are designed with exceptional care down to the last detail. Furniture by cutting-edge designers is combined with classic features to create a harmonious ensemble. Bold graphics, unusual textiles and retro-styled wallpaper decorate the walls of the hotel rooms and public spaces. Whether the design is a playful, decorative floral or dense pattern of yellow checks, every one of the wallpapers has its own identity. The designers have ensured that the guestrooms and conference areas make the best use of their walls, creating an atmosphere of space and freedom, executed in a clean, unobtrusive style. Unique design objects and graphics give every room its own special charm.

25hours Hotel

Zeitgemäßes Design, ein individueller Stil und guter Service zu moderaten Übernachtungspreisen: dieses Konzept findet sich beim 25hours Hotel überall wieder. Die 95 Zimmer und sieben Suiten sind außergewöhnlich und mit viel Liebe zum Detail gestaltet. Möbel junger Designer werden mit Klassikern zu einem harmonischen Ensemble kombiniert. Großflächige Grafiken, ungewöhnliche Textzeilen oder Retro-Tapeten zieren die Wände der Zimmer und öffentlichen Räumlichkeiten. Ob verspielt und mit dekorativen Blumenmustern ausgestattet oder gelbe Vichykaros – die Tapeten haben alle ihre eigene Identität. Die Zimmer und Studios im 25hours Hotel bieten Raum und Freiheit, einen unaufdringlich klaren Stil und ein Maximum an Wandlungsfähigkeit. Einzigartige Designobjekte und Grafiken geben jedem Zimmer seinen besonderen Charme.

25hours Hôtel

Design contemporain, style personnalisé, service de qualité à des prix modérés : ces concepts s'imposent partout au 25hours Hôtel. On y trouve 95 chambres et sept suites toutes décorées avec originalité et amour du détail. Des meubles de jeunes créateurs se marient à du mobilier ancien et forment des ensembles harmonieux. Panneaux graphiques, motifs insolites et papiers peints rétro décorent les murs des chambres et des espaces publics. Qu'ils soient kitsch et décorés de motifs floraux ou en vinyle à carreaux jaunes, les papiers peints se distinguent tous par leur caractère unique. Les chambres et suites du 25hours Hôtel sont spacieuses et offrent une impression de liberté, un style net et sobre, et des possibilités de transformations multiples. Des objets design recherchés avec soin et des lithographies donnent à chaque chambre un charme qui lui est propre.

Each guestroom is individually decorated with modern furniture and nostalgic wallpaper.

Die Gästezimmer sind individuell im Retro-Stil mit modernen Möbeln und nostalgischen Tapeten eingerichtet.

Style rétro individuel pour des chambres équipées d'un mobilier moderne rehaussé par des papiers peints de facture nostalgique.

Sharp, clearly defined patterns add character to a room.

Markante Muster prägen den Raum mit ihrem Charakter.

Des papiers peints surprenant personnalisent l'espace.

Artists Delphine Buhro and Michael Dreher spent over a year scouring flea markets, trade shows and forgotten wallpaper archives. Their creations reflect an eclectic mixture of art, design and cultural history.

Die Künstler Delphine Buhro und Michael Dreher haben über ein Jahr Design-Messen, vergessene Tapetenlager und Flohmärkte durchforstet und eine eklektische Mischung aus Kunst, Design und Kulturgeschichte geschaffen.

Pendant plus d'une année, les artistes Delphine Buhro et Michael Dreher ont hanté les salons de design, fouillé les entrepôts de tapisserie et les marchés aux puces pour réaliser un mélange éclectique d'art, de design et d'histoire des civilisations.

Luigi Colani

Water Waves

Luigi Colani, long the "enfant terrible" of the design scene, has also produced his own collection of wallpaper. The knowledge that all life began in water led to the basic idea behind the extraordinary Water Waves. Water in all its different forms, from droplets to rushing waves, is at the heart of each design. Complex technical innovations had to be developed in order to realize Colani's extraordinary vision. The integral interference glitter produces pronounced iridescent effects. The colors vary strongly and are constantly changing when viewed from different angles, resembling the light-reflecting, shimmering surface of water.

Water Waves

Luigi Colani, das „enfant terrible" der Designszene, hat eine eigene Tapetenkollektion entworfen. Aus der Erkenntnis, dass alles Leben aus dem Wasser kommt, formulierte er die Grundidee für die außergewöhnliche Kollektion. Wasser in all seinen Erscheinungsformen, vom Tropfen bis zu fließenden Wellenformationen bilden die Basis seiner Dessins. Aufwändige technische Innovationen waren nötig um die außergewöhnlichen Tapeten zu realisieren. Der eingesetzte Interferenzglimmer zeigt einen ausgeprägten Flip-Flop-Effekt. Die Farben changieren stark und verändern sich mit dem Betrachtungswinkel. Sie wecken Assoziationen mit einer Licht reflektierenden, schimmernden Wasseroberfläche.

Water Waves

Luigi Colani, l'« enfant terrible » du design a conçu sa propre gamme de papiers peints baptisée *Water Waves*. L'idée de base de cette collection très originale est que toute vie vient de l'eau. L'eau sous toutes ses formes, de la goutte à la vague déferlante, constitue le motif de ses dessins. L'élaboration de ces papiers peints exceptionnels s'est effectuée à l'aide d'innovations techniques de pointe. Les nuances micacées interférentielles produisent un effet « flip-flop » accentué. Les couleurs changent complètement selon l'angle de vue de l'observateur. Elles évoquent des associations avec des surfaces d'eau scintillantes où se reflète la lumière.

A highlight of the collection is the shimmering matte pearls glued to bands of color running through the wallpaper, adding an air of noble refinement.

Das innovative Highlight der Kollektion sind matt schimmernde Perlen, die auf Tapetenbahnen appliziert werden und einen Look edler Raffinesse schaffen.

Clou de la collection : les perles nacrées mates appliquées sur les pans de tapisserie qui apportent noblesse et raffinement à l'ensemble.

New to the collection are droplets that can be attached to wallpaper or window drapes.

Neu sind auch Dekorelemente in zwei Tropfenformen, die vom Verbraucher frei auf die Tapetenbahnen und die passend dazu angebotenen Flächenvorhänge appliziert werden können.

Inédits, ces deux éléments en forme de gouttes d'eau peuvent s'appliquer en laissant libre cours à sa fantaisie sur le papier peint et les rideaux assortis.

Dominic Crinson

Roses, Sapphire #5

Individualized wall and floor treatments are the primary business of the English design firm Digitile. Working together with architects and designers like Dominic Crinson, Digitile provides residences, shops, restaurants and bars with one of a kind decor using made to measure printed wallpaper. The Betty Barclay shop on London's Oxford Street was the result of a close collaboration between interior designer and architect. In order to best convey the image of the brand, the rose was chosen as a symbol of femininity. The photographer Nick Miller was called in to capture the image of the rose in all its shining glory. Blown up to enormous size, printed on paper and mounted on wall panels, the picture of a sparkling rose now decorates the retail space.

Roses, Sapphire #5

Die individuelle Gestaltung von Wand- oder Bodenfliesen und Tapeten ist das Hauptgeschäft des englischen Unternehmens Digitile. In Zusammenarbeit mit Architekten und Designern wie Dominic Crinson werden private Wohnungen und Interiors von Shops, Restaurants oder Bars mit Hilfe der maßgeschneiderten Drucke zu Unikaten. Für den Betty Barclay Shop in der Londoner Oxford Street arbeiteten sie mit den für die Umgestaltung zuständigen Architekten eng zusammen. Um den Stil der Marke zu repräsentieren, entschied man sich dafür eine Rose als Symbol von Weiblichkeit und Eleganz zu inszenieren. Mit dem Photographen Nick Miller wurde ein Partner gefunden, der die Rose in ihrer ganzen leuchtenden Pracht einfangen konnte. Großflächig auf Wandpaneele aufgezogen, schmückt das Bild einer strahlend roten Rose nun die Verkaufsräume.

Roses, Sapphire #5

La société anglaise Digitile est spécialisée dans le carrelage personnalisé de murs et de sols, ainsi que dans la tapisserie. En collaboration avec des architectes et créateurs tels que Dominic Crinson, des lieux d'habitations, des magasins, restaurants et bars acquièrent une physionomie unique grâce à des décors élaborés sur mesure. Pour le magasin londonien Betty Barclay situé sur Oxford Street, Dominic Crinson a travaillé en étroite collaboration avec les architectes chargés de la transformation de l'édifice. Symbole de la féminité et de l'élégance, la rose a été choisie comme ambassadrice de la marque. Le photographe Nick Miller a donné à la fleur tout son éclat et sa beauté. Décorant de vastes panneaux muraux, de magnifiques roses rouges rehaussent divers rayons du magasin.

Predominantly blue hues were used in this children's room. Chocolate brown, red and orange accents delineate the delicate balance between clean lines and rustic shading. The wallpaper Sapphire #5 expressively underlines the playful spirit of the room.

Das Kinderzimmer ist überwiegend in blauen Farbtönen gehalten, Akzente von Braun-, Rot- und Orangetönen betonen eine zarte Balance aus klaren Linien und rustikaler Abstufung. Die Tapete „Sapphire #5" unterstreicht eindrucksvoll die spielerische Stimmung des Raumes.

Diverses nuances de bleus dominent dans cette chambre d'enfant. Des tons chocolat, rouge et orange soulignent l'équilibre délicat entre lignes pures et éléments rustiques. La tapisserie *Sapphire #5* rehausse l'ambiance ludique de la pièce.

Hotel Fox

As late as 2004, the Hotel Fox, at that time still the Park-Hotel, was full of heavy oak furnishings, chandeliers and dark carpeting. The desire for a new interior led to the idea of creating a uniquely decorative hotel. Instead of a unified design schematic, each room would be furnished and decorated by a different artist. Out of more than 3000 applicants, 21 designers were chosen to work on the renovation. The hotel building was cleaned and emptied of all furniture. The artists were assigned to rooms with plain, white walls. Design went off in a number of different directions, some strange and provocative, others edgy and inspirational. In addition to the rooms with painted walls, 32 were decorated with new wallpaper. No room or pattern was the same as any other.

Hotel Fox

Noch Ende 2004 gab es im Hotel Fox, das zu dem Zeitpunkt noch Park-Hotel hieß, schwere Eichenmöbel, Kronleuchter und dunklen Teppichboden. Nun wollte man ein neues Interieur, daraus entstand die Idee ein einzigartiges Hotel zu schaffen, in dem jedes Zimmer von einem anderen Künstler gestaltet werden sollte. Unter mehr als 3000 Bewerbern wurden schließlich die 21 ausgewählt, die an der Umsetzung beteiligt waren. Komplett leer geräumt und saniert, wurden den Künstlern die Zimmer mit komplett weißen Wänden übergeben. Entstanden sind vielfältige Inszenierungen, seltsam, provozierend, aufregend und inspirierend. Neben gemalten Unikaten sind auch 32 neue Tapeten entstanden. Kein Zimmer und kein Muster gleicht dem anderen.

Hôtel Fox

Fin 2004, un lourd mobilier en chêne, des lustres et des moquettes sombres décoraient encore l'hôtel Fox, alors appelé Park-Hotel. Quand il fut question d'en changer la décoration, l'idée naquit de créer un hôtel exceptionnel, dans lequel chaque chambre serait aménagée par un artiste et serait donc unique. Parmi plus de 3 000 candidatures, 21 furent retenues pour participer à l'aventure. Entièrement vidé de ses meubles et réhabilité, tous ses murs peints en blanc, l'hôtel fut remis aux mains des artistes. Au final, l'ensemble est d'une grande diversité avec des aménagements et des décors insolites, provocants, excitants et suggestifs. Aux œuvres peintes en un seul exemplaire s'ajoutent 32 tapisseries inédites créées à cette occasion. Aucune pièce et aucun décor ne se ressemblent.

Geneviève Gauckler creates colorful, kaleidoscopic, computer-generated dream worlds.

Geneviève Gauckler kreiert farbenfrohe, kaleidoskopische, am Computer gestaltete Traum-welten.

Geneviève Gauckler élabore sur son ordinateur des univers irréels, kaléidoscopiques et colorés.

The decorative scheme created by the London design group Container is playful, romantic and atmospheric.

Die Gestaltung der Londoner Designgruppe Container ist verspielt, romantisch und voller Atmosphäre.

Les designers londoniens du groupe Container créent des ambiances romantiques, ludiques et chaleureuses.

Deuce Design

Interior Design Projects

Deuce Design is a multidisciplinary design studio offering the full palette of creative services: business logos; environmental graphics, large format graphics; printing services; marketing and web design. Deuce Design analyzes a client's image, supplies a design solution, and stays involved throughout as an interdisciplinary advisor. The company relies on a network of strong partnerships with architects, interior designers, and landscape architects. One part of the studio's work involves the production of individualized, handmade wallpaper for any lifestyle or functional space, from bars and clubs to flower shops.

Projekte Innenarchitektur

Deuce Design ist ein fachübergreifendes Design Studio mit der kompletten Palette von kreativen Dienstleistungen wie Corporate Design, Umwelt- und Großformatgraphik, Druckbegleitung, Kommunikation und Web Design. Deuce Design analysieren das Erscheinungsbild ihrer Kunden, verleihen ihm Gestalt und verstehen sich ganzheitlich als interdisziplinäre Berater. Dabei spielt ihr weltweites Netzwerk eine wichtige Rolle im kreativen Entwicklungsprozess. Ein Netzwerk welches auf starke Partnerschaften mit Architekten, Innenarchitekten und Landschaftsarchitekten basiert. Ein Teil der kreativen Arbeit des Studios liegt inzwischen auch in der Gestaltung von individuellen und handgefertigten Tapeten für fast alle Lebens- und Einsatzbereiche – von Bars über Clubs bis hin zu Blumenläden.

Projets d'architecture intérieure

Deuce Design est une société qui regroupe plusieurs secteurs d'activités et offre une palette complète de prestations dans le domaine créatif : le corporate design, l'illustration grand format, l'impression, la communication, la stratégie et le Web design. Deuce Design étudie les éléments qui composent l'identité de ses clients et lui donne une forme. Société de conseil interdisciplinaire, l'entreprise s'appuie sur un réseau dont l'importance est primordiale dans le processus de création. Ce réseau repose sur de solides partenariats avec des architectes, architectes d'intérieur et architectes-paysagistes. Parmi les activités de Deuce Design, on trouve également l'élaboration de papiers peints personnalisés, fabriqués manuellement et destinés à presque tous les espaces privés et publics – des bars aux clubs, jusqu'aux boutiques de fleuristes.

Wallpaper is the perfect platform for patterns derived from contemporary graphic design.

Die Muster werden sehr nahe an das Graphikdesign angelehnt und Tapeten liefern die perfekte Plattform für deren Umsetzung.

Les motifs s'inspirent de l'art graphique auquel le papier peint offre un support idéal.

The opening of a new Hotel is always an exciting occasion. In addition to business accessories like stationary, business cards and brochures, unique wallpapers were created for the public spaces of the Hotel Central.

Hoteleröffnungen sind eine spannende Sache. Neben der Geschäftsausstattung mit Briefbögen, Visitenkarten und Hotelprospekten wurden auch individuelle Tapetenentwürfe für die öffentlichen Räume des Hotel Central realisiert.

L'ouverture d'un nouvel hôtel est une chose grisante. Parallèlement à la création de papier à lettres, cartes de visites et dépliants, des panneaux muraux exceptionnels ont été réalisés pour les espaces de réception de l'Hôtel Central.

Design Object Wallpapers

Wallpaper murals are now recognized as an exceptionally adaptable decor element for the interior design of business offices, retail stores, medical practices, hospitals and private residences as well. The wallpaper murals produced by the Berlin firm DrNice are well known as the largest, most emphatic examples available. There are photographic murals, the newly developed non-woven wallpapers with bold, graphic designs, children's wallpapers and borders, literature collages by the poet Herta Müller, and also wallpapers that help bring a living space in synch with the principles of Feng Shui. DrNice designs decorate walls beautifully and coherently, giving each space its own individual, always stimulating character.

Tapetenobjekte

Bildtapeten entwickeln sich zu einem außergewöhnlichen und vielseitig einsetzbarem Gestaltungselement bei der Einrichtung von Unternehmen, Ladengeschäften, Arztpraxen, Krankenhäusern oder auch privaten Haushalten. Die Bildtapeten des Berliner Herstellers DrNice sind bewusst als große, Akzente setzende, Wandbilder konzipiert. Es gibt sie als Fototapete, als Vliestapeten mit großen, grafischen Designs, als Kindertapeten und Borten fürs Kinderzimmer, Literaturtapeten mit Collagen von Herta Müller oder auch als Tapeten, die helfen, den Lebensraum in Einklang mit den Elementen nach Feng Shui zu gestalten – alle bekleiden die Wände auf stimmige, schöne Art und Weise und geben dem Raum immer wieder einen spannenden, individuellen Charakter.

Panneaux décoratifs

Les panneaux décoratifs sont de plus en plus prisés comme des éléments originaux et polyvalents dans l'aménagement de l'espace, qu'il s'agisse d'entreprises, de magasins, de cabinets médicaux et d'hôpitaux, ou d'habitat individuel. Les panneaux décoratifs du fabricant berlinois DrNice sont conçus pour former des tableaux muraux grand format qui caractérisent l'espace dans lequel ils se trouvent. Papier peint panoramique, papier peint textile décoré de grands motifs graphiques, papier peint et frises ludiques pour les chambres d'enfant, papier peint « littéraire » avec collages de Herta Müller ou encore papier peint s'intégrant dans un espace aménagé selon les règles du Feng Shui, tous ces panneaux tapissent admirablement les murs et donnent aux espaces un caractère original et individuel.

Wallpaper murals—individualized messages on walls.

Bildtapeten – individuelle Bildbotschaften an Wänden.

Panneaux décoratifs – des messages personnels sur les murs.

Perspective and information communicated symbolically, united in a wallpaper design.

Perspektiven und symbolische Botschaften vereint in einem Tapetenmotiv.

Perspectives et symboles réunis dans un panneau décoratif.

In addition to wallpaper murals, DrNice creates decorative plastic film for all or part of a car's exterior. These can be made to order according to the client's wishes, or ordered from one of the firm's special collections. The design Amazon Jungle from the Paradise and Oasis collection adorns both the car and the walls of this sharp showroom.

Zusätzlich zu den Bildtapeten kreierte DrNice Folien für Fahrzeuge aller Art, die individuell nach den Wünschen der Kunden bedruckt werden können. Für den smart wurde eine ganz spezielle Kollektion von großflächigen Mustern entwickelt. Amazonas Jungle aus der Kollektion „Paradiese und Oasen" schmückt diesen Wagen und die Wände des smart Showroom.

Au-delà des panneaux décoratifs, DrNice personnalise les voitures en créant un revêtement décoratif qui répond aux attentes du client. Pour la Smart, la société a élaboré une collection qui s'appuie sur de grands motifs. Élément de la collection *Paradis et océans,* le motif *Jungle amazonienne* décore cette voiture et les murs de la salle où elle est exposée.

endless wallpaper

buzzer

The wallpapers created by designer Bettina Dirkes pay homage to life and nature, giving a room a positive atmosphere that carries over to everyone in it. The distinctive buzzer wallpaper collection engages the senses with its powerful effects. The motifs captivate with their energetic colors, creating unique accents through their lovingly executed details. Large format wall images set the mood for private spaces, bars, boutiques and discriminating retail establishments like hotels, reception halls and restaurants. Dirkes' work differs from conventional wallpaper in that the large format motif extends over several rolls, with few formal constraints.

buzzer

Die Tapeten der Gestalterin Bettina Dirkes sind eine Hommage an das Leben und die Natur. Sie sollen Räumen eine positive Grundstimmung geben, die sich auf den Betrachter überträgt. Endless Wallpapers ist eine außergewöhnliche Tapetenkollektion, die faszinierend sinnlich und dennoch kraftvoll erscheint. Die Motive bestechen durch energische Farben und setzen einzigartige Akzente mit liebevollen, gestalterischen Details. Großformatige Wandbilder betonen private Räumlichkeiten, Bars, Boutiquen und exquisite Läden, sowie Hotels, Empfangshallen und Restaurants. Sie unterscheiden sich von herkömmlichen Tapeten, da sich das Motiv über mehrere Bahnen erstreckt und nicht rapportiert ist.

buzzer

Les papiers peints du designer Bettina Dirkes rendent hommage à la vie et à la nature. Ils créent une ambiance positive dont s'imprègne l'observateur. *Buzzer* de la société endless wallpaper est une collection exceptionnelle de papiers peints à la sensualité fascinante et aux lignes très expressives. Les motifs aux couleurs vives apportent des accents uniques grâce à des détails décoratifs pensés avec soin. Les panneaux muraux grand format ornent avec raffinement espaces d'habitation, bars, boutiques de luxe, hôtels, halls de réception et restaurants. À la différence du papier peint traditionnel, le motif s'étend sur plusieurs pans et n'a pas de format fixé au préalable.

Wallpaper from the wide variety of collections can be cut to order according to a client's individual needs. The material is a high-quality, robust fleece composed of a blend of textile and cellulose fibers. Special finishing ensures that the colors remain bold and fresh even in strong light.

Die Tapeten aus der varianten-reichen Kollektion werden für den Käufer individuell und maß-gerecht gefertigt. Das Material ist ein hochwertiges, extrem strapazierfähiges Vlies aus Textil- und Zellulosefasern. Eine speziel-le Veredlung stellt sicher, dass die Farben selbst bei starker Lichtein-strahlung dauerhaft frisch und kräftig bleiben.

La collection propose un riche choix de papiers peints fabriqués sur mesure selon les besoins des clients. Le matériau utilisé est de grande qualité et consiste en un mélange très résistant de fibres de cellulose et de fibres textiles. Grâce à un traitement spécial, les couleurs conservent leur fraîcheur et leur éclat, même lorsqu'elles sont exposées à une forte luminosité.

Front Design

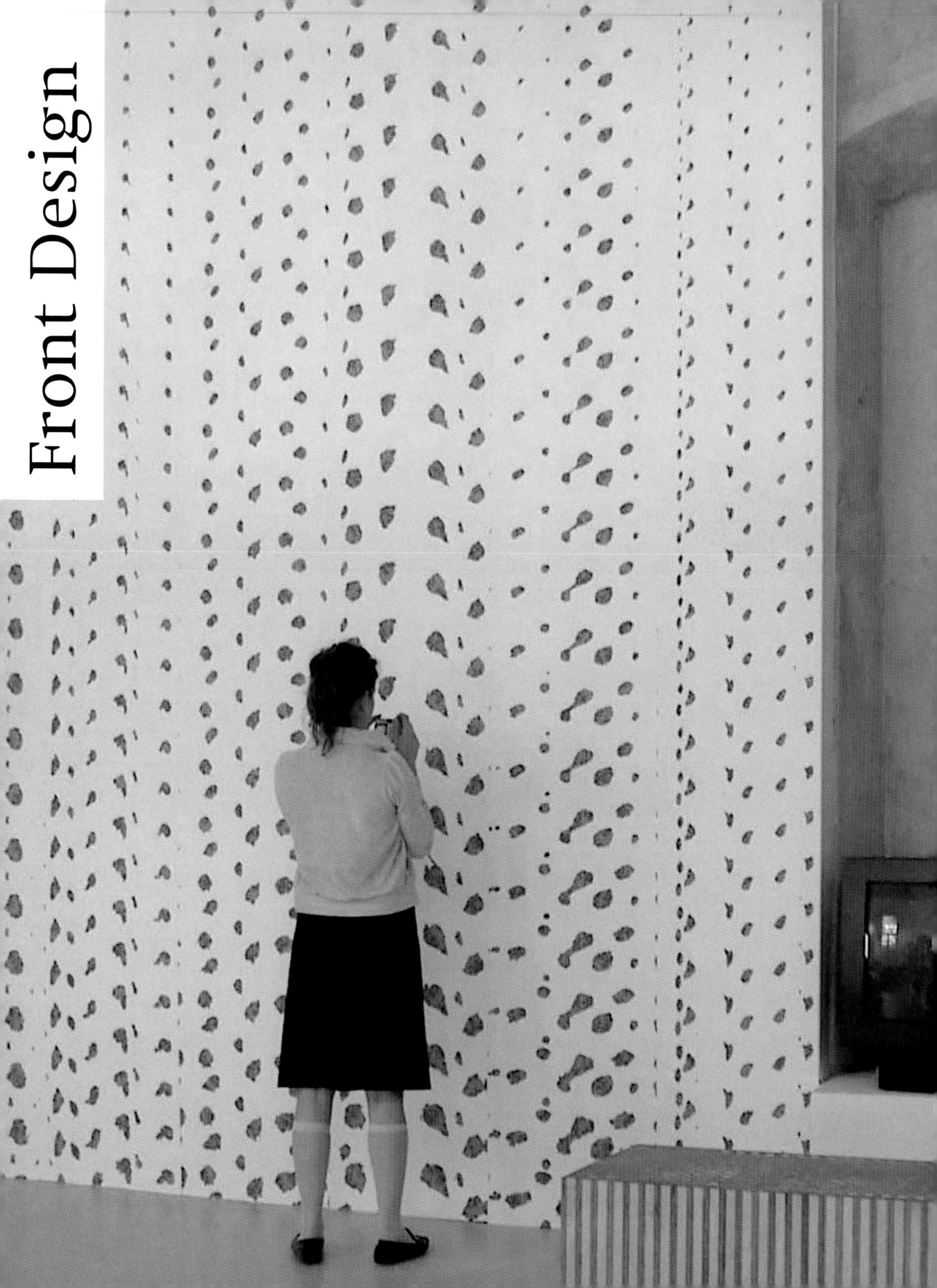

Rats and Wallpaper

Sofia Lagerkvist, Katja Sävström, Charlotte von der Lancken and Anna Lindgren met each other at the Konstfack School of Arts, Crafts and Design in Stockholm, Sweden, where they now run an international design studio. Their motto "furnishings to fall in love with at first sight, or hate forever" perfectly expresses the polarizing effect of their designs. Kitsch, poetry, provocation and experimentation are a given in their Stockholm studio. Their love of innovation was rewarded with the Designer of the Future prize at the 2007 Design Miami/ Basel trade fair. Their design office combines their many years of professional experience in different fields with spontaneity, strategic marketing skills, productive restlessness and results-oriented creativity.

Tapete und Ratten

Sofia Lagerkvist, Katja Sävström, Charlotte von der Lancken und Anna Lindgren haben sich an der Konstfack School of Arts, Crafts & Design kennen gelernt und betreiben mit Front Design ein internationales Designbüro in Kopenhagen. Ihr Credo „Furniture to fall in love with at first sight, or hate forever" ist Programm: Design, das polarisiert. Kitsch, Poesie, Provokation, Experimente sind angesagt im Stockholmer Design-Lab. Ihre Innovationsfreude wurde mit dem Award „Designer of the Future" auf der Design Miami/Basel ausgezeichnet. In ihrem Designbüro verbinden sich langjährige Berufserfahrung aus verschiedenen Branchen mit spontanem und strategischem Denken, produktiver Unruhe und ergebnisorientierter Kreativität.

Tapisserie et rats

Sofia Lagerkvist, Katja Sävström, Charlotte von der Lancken et Anna Lindgren se sont rencontrées à la Konstfack School of Arts, Crafts & Design et exploitent ensemble Front Design, agence de design internationale basée à Copenhague. Leur programme suit le credo : « Furniture to fall in love with at first sight, or hate forever » (du mobilier dont on s'éprend au premier regard ou qu'on hait à jamais). Il va sans dire que leur design soulève la controverse. Kitsch, poésie, provocation, expérimentation sont autant de facettes de leur travail dans le laboratoire à idées de Stockholm. Cette ardeur innovatrice leur a valu le prix du « Designer of the Future » à l'exposition Design Miami/Basel. Front Design associe de longues années d'expérience dans divers secteurs à une réflexion à la fois spontanée et stratégique, à une effervescence féconde et à une créativité pragmatique.

Searching for new means of expression, the designers chose wallpaper as the medium with which to convey their message. Their series Rat Wallpaper took pieces of old and new wallpaper, and gave them to rats to chew on. The chance arrangement of the gnawed holes served as the basis of the wallpaper pattern.

Auf der Suche nach neuen Ausdrucksmitteln haben Designer die Tapete als Medium ihrer Botschaften entdeckt. Bei „Rat Wallpaper" werden alte und neue Tapeten durch Ratten angefressen. Die auf diese Weise nach dem Zufallsprinzip entstehenden Löcher bilden die Grundlage eines neuen Tapetenmusters.

À la recherche de nouveaux moyens d'expression, les designers ont découvert le papier peint comme « médium ». Le rat wallpaper, c'est-à-dire du papier peint neuf ou vieux grignoté par des rats, est une de leur création. Les trous obtenus au hasard constituent la base d'un nouveau motif de papier peint.

gohome

Octopus, Caviar and Lobster

The idea behind this newly founded brand for modern urban living is as follows: there will always be moments in life in which it is preferable to withdraw to one's own home either because it is raining, the night was long or the hustle and bustle of the world outside has simply become too much. So far, gohome's design collections have consisted solely of wallpaper, and very unique wallpaper at that. The wallpaper is produced by means of the most up-to-date, digital printing techniques in combination with innovative materials and traditional workmanship. Each completed collection has its own development history originating with an idea from its maker. The Neo-Baroque wallpaper from the Anakron series reveals its secret upon a second look. Images representing the themes of the wallpaper's namesake, the poet Anakron, a man famous for his verses on wine, women, friendship and love, are integrated into what at first glance looks like a conventional motif.

Oktopus, Kaviar, Hummer

Die Idee des neu gegründeten Labels für modernes urbanes Wohnen: Es gibt immer Momente im Leben, in denen es besser ist, sich in sein Heim zurückzuziehen – ganz gleich, ob es ein verregneter Tag ist, die Nacht zuvor zu lang war oder der allgemeine Trubel in der Welt zu nervig wird. Bisher umfasst die Kollektion nur Tapeten, diese jedoch sind einzigartig. Die Produktion erfolgt in modernster, digitaler Drucktechnik in Kombination mit innovativen Materialien und in einer für Tapeten traditionellen Art der Weiterverarbeitung. Sie haben alle ihre eigene Entstehungsgeschichte und entstammen den Ideen der Macher. Die neo-barock anmutende Tapete der Serie „Anakron" enthüllt erst beim zweiten Blick ihr Geheimnis: Da der Namensgeber Dichter war, dessen Themen Freundschaft, Frauen, Wein und Eros waren, verbinden sich diese Figuren zu einem zeitgemäßen Muster.

Poulpe, caviar, homard

Récemment créé, le label spécialisé dans l'habitat citadin moderne a pour credo le constat suivant : il existe des moments dans la vie où il vaut mieux s'enfermer chez soi – que ce soit parce qu'il fait mauvais temps, que la nuit passée a été trop longue ou encore parce qu'on ne supporte plus les problèmes du monde. Jusqu'à présent, gohome ne propose que des papiers peints, mais ils n'ont pas leurs pareils. La production du papier peint s'opère avec les techniques numériques d'impression les plus modernes, associées à des matériaux inédits et aux méthodes traditionnelles de finissage. Chaque papier peint a sa propre histoire et est le fruit de l'imagination d'un créateur. Le papier peint néobaroque de la série *Anakron* ne révèle son secret qu'après y avoir porté l'attention qu'il mérite. Il porte en effet le nom d'un poète dont les sujets d'inspiration – amitié, femmes, vin et Éros – sont réunis au sein d'un motif contemporain.

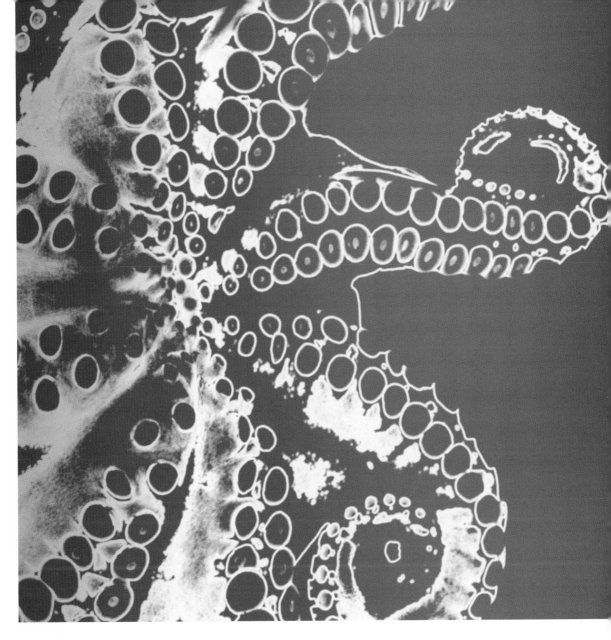

The motifs unite modern images with ornamental elements from traditional wallpaper. As has always been true, over time the changing aesthetic makes itself felt, even in wallpaper design.

Das Motiv vereint ein modernes Bild mit ornamentalen Elementen eines traditionellen Tapetendesigns. Wie auch immer, im Laufe der Zeit kristallisiert sich so auch im Tapetendesign eine veränderte Ästhetik heraus.

Voici un motif moderne qui reprend toutefois des éléments ornementaux tirés d'un papier peint traditionnel. La tapisserie prend acte des évolutions esthétiques en cours.

The photographs used in the
Lobster wallpaper were shot in
the wallpaper studio in Cologne
(Germany).

Das Foto der Hummertapete
wurde direkt in der Tapetenagentur in Köln aufgenommen.

Le cliché du papier peint représentant des homards a été pris dans
les bureaux du label, à Cologne.

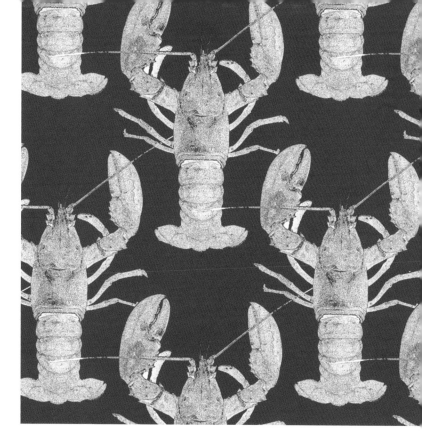

This homey design is ideal
for the kitchen or dining area.
Bon Appetit!

Diese heimische Produktion
ist optimal für die Küche
oder den Essbereich geeignet.
Guten Appetit!

Ce papier peint est tout à fait
approprié à la décoration de
cuisines ou de salles à manger.
Bon appétit !

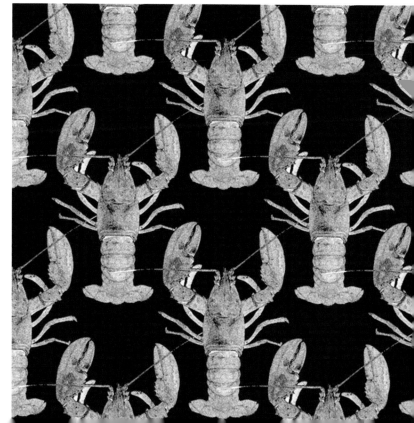

ippolito fleitz group

Da Loretta

Peter Ippolito and Gunter Fleitz run a multidisciplinary, internationally renowned design studio in Stuttgart. Working together with the textile designer Monika Trenkler, the firm has developed wallpaper designs that set twentieth century middle class wallpaper alongside contemporary motifs and scanned, digitized images of wood grain. In the restaurant Trattoria Da Loretta, this wall treatment combined with text is virtually a spatial representation of the Renaissance poem Quant' è bella giovinezza by Lorenzo II de Medici. Fragments of the text of the poem are scattered through the room, in corners, behind mirrors, under the bar and in gaps in the ceiling. Enlarged scans of lace doilies filled in with copper colored inlays are used in place of the plaster rosettes one would normally find around lighting fixtures.

Da Loretta

Peter Ippolito und Gunter Fleitz betreiben ein multidisziplinäres, international tätiges Studio für Gestaltung in Stuttgart. In Zusammenarbeit mit der Textildesignerin Monika Trenkler wurden für die Gestaltung Tapetenstreifen entwickelt, bei denen sich bürgerliche Tapeten vergangener Jahrhunderte, zeitgenössische Muster, sowie gescannte und digital ausbelichtete Holztexturen nebeneinander stellen. In der Trattoria wird das Renaissancegedicht ‚Quant' è bella giovinezza ...‘ von Lorenzo Il Magnifico räumlich inszeniert. Fragmente des Textes finden sich in Raumecken, Spiegeln, unter dem Tresen oder in Deckenaussparungen. Vergrößerte Scans von Spitzendeckchen, aufgemalt mit kupferfarbenem Hammerschlag, ersetzen an der Decke rund um die Lampen die nicht vorhandenen Stuckrosetten.

Da Loretta

Peter Ippolito et Gunter Fleitz dirigent une agence d'architecture d'intérieur multidisciplinaire et internationale située à Stuttgart. En collaboration avec Monika Trenkler, spécialisée dans le design textile, ils ont élaboré un décor où se succèdent des bandes formées de papiers peints des siècles passés, des motifs contemporains, des textures de bois scannées et travaillées numériquement. Dans la Trattoria Da Loretta, le poème Renaissance *Quant' è bella giovinezza ...* de Laurence Il le Magnifique a été mis en scène. On retrouve des citations du texte dans les coins de la salle, sur les miroirs, sur le comptoir et à certains endroits du plafond. Des napperons en dentelle scannés dont la couleur est semblable au cuivre martelé remplacent les stucs manquant autour des lustres.

Nature and its consummate integration of aesthetics and function are the ideas that form the basis of this wall treatment. An easily decipherable pictorial language develops out of the organic forms of flowers and plants. Interspersed throughout is the gently bowed circle that serves as the logo of the clinic, but also as a symbol of the search for beauty undertaken by every individual. Upon entering the medical practice offices, the visitor is greeted by this key visual element painted on a wall behind the reception desk. The blue dot signals arrival and the clinic logo fits quite naturally into the floral motif. The dynamic, boldly designed reception area breaks the symmetry in front of the wall. In contrast to the high gloss reflective lacquer of the central island wall treatment, the walls on the opposite side of the hallway utilize warm hues and natural materials.

Die Natur und ihre vollkommene Verbindung von Ästhetik und Funktion bilden die Grundideen der Wandgestaltung. Aus organischen Formen, Blüten oder Pflanzen entstand eine eigenständige Bildsprache, mit hohem Wiedererkennungswert. Hinzu kommt ein leicht verformter Kreis, der als Markenzeichen der Klinik fungiert, sowie als Symbol für die Suche nach individuell gefühlter Schönheit steht. Beim Eintreten in die Praxis wird der Besucher vom „Key Visual" der Praxis, der Bemalung der Mittelinsel, willkommen geheißen. Der blaue Punkt signalisiert das Ankommen. Das Logo der Klinik fügt sich selbstverständlich in das florale Motiv ein. Vor der Wand steht die dynamisch geformte, die Symmetrie aufbrechende Rezeption. Sie ist, im Gegensatz zur reflektierenden Lackoberfläche der Mittelinsel, in warmen Materialien und Farbtönen gehalten.

Cet aménagement mural allie esthétique et fonction de manière parfaite, à l'image de la nature qu'il reproduit. Des éléments organiques, fleurs ou plantes, forment un langage visuel caractéristique. S'y ajoute un cercle légèrement déformé qui sert de logo à la clinique, mais qui est aussi le symbole d'une recherche de beauté individuelle. En entrant dans la clinique, le visiteur est accueilli par le leitmotiv du lieu, la décoration de l'îlot central. Le cercle bleu en signale l'entrée. Le logo de la clinique s'insère naturellement dans le motif floral. Placée devant ce logo, la réception et ses lignes dynamiques casse la symétrie de l'entrée. Le meuble est réalisé à partir de matériaux et de tons chauds qui contrastent avec les surfaces laquées et réfléchissantes de l'espace qui l'entoure.

Unter dieser Blutbuche zu liegen,
mmer bei heller Sonne.
das Licht von oben
rch die dunklen Blätter scheint, dann sind s
ot, brennen, leuchten, flammen auf.
dann schließe ich meine Augen und denke m
roten, vollen Lippen
dicht vor mein Gesicht.

The plant motifs on the lacquered side of the hallway are complemented by carefully chosen texts on the subject of aesthetics and function written on the blue wall opposite. Text and wall paintings are organized so as to support the activities that take place in each space.

Das Pflanzenmotiv auf der lackierten Seite wird durch ausgewählte Texte zum Thema „Ästhetik und Funktion" auf der blauen Wand komplettiert. Sowohl Texte als auch Wandbemalung sind so angeordnet, dass sie die unterschiedlichen räumlichen Situationen unterstützen.

Le motif floral est complété sur un autre mur par des textes choisis sur le thème « esthétique et fonction ». Textes et motifs peints sont agencés de manière à souligner la fonction des différents espaces.

Apartment S

The architects and designers of ippolito fleitz group do work that spans many different creative fields. Thus, artists are always being called in to advise on individual projects with the goal of producing something unmistakably special. In the private residence Apartment S, it is the extraordinarily feminine ceiling decoration that draws the most attention. Designed by Monica Trenkler, the ceiling motifs continue throughout the entire apartment, unifying the different living areas. In the bathroom, textiles made from Corian® are molded to the walls, drawing the eye of anyone standing under the showerhead. Dark furnishings serve as a contrast to the colorfully decorated walls. Cozy corner seating, individualized accessories and high quality designer furniture speak of the exclusive tastes of the owner.

Wohnung S

Die Architekten und Designer der Ippolito Fleitz Gruppe arbeiten branchenübergreifend und es werden immer wieder Künstler bei den unterschiedlichen Projekten zu Rate gezogen, um etwas Unverwechselbares zu schaffen. Vor allem die außergewöhnliche feminine, florale Deckenillustration lenkt die Aufmerksamkeit auf sich. Gestaltet von Monica Trenkler, zieht sie sich durch die gesamte Wohnung und verbindet die verschiedenen Bereiche. In den Bädern sind Textzeilen in die Wände aus Corian® eingefräst und ziehen beim Duschen unter der Regendusche die Blicke auf sich. Dunkle Möbel, sowie der dunkle Boden bilden einen Kontrast mit den farbig gestalteten Wänden. Heimelige Sitzecken, individuelle Accessoires und hochwertige Designermöbel zeugen vom exklusiven Geschmack der Bewohner.

Appartement S

Les architectes et designers du groupe ippolito fleitz travaillent de manière interdisciplinaire faisant souvent appel à d'autres artistes et designers afin de créer des ouvrages uniques. Ici, le regard est surtout attiré par la décoration florale très féminine du plafond. Réalisée par Monica Trenkler, elle se retrouve sur tous les plafonds de l'appartement et relie les divers espaces. Dans les salles de bains, des motifs sont gravés sur les murs recouverts de corian ; ils se dévoilent sous le jet de la douche. Un mobilier de bois sombre et les sols également foncés forment un contraste avec les murs aux couleurs vives. De superbes canapés, des accessoires recherchés et des meubles design haut de gamme témoignent du goût très sûr du propriétaire du lieu.

T-012

The name is not only a synonym for the address of the nightclub, but a reference to a famous Stuttgart citizen: Theodore Heuss, the first President of the Federal Republic of Germany. In his honor, a selection of quotes made famous by this rakish, good-humored bon vivant has been written on the stairway walls. The color scheme for every room is black and white throughout. Mirrors and large-scale illustrations increase the impact of the space. Adhesive, polarized plastic film covers the ground floor window. During the day, it reflects the silhouette of the city. Evenings, when the club is lit from within, the silhouette motif disappears, giving way to view of the free-standing, U-shaped bar made of white Corian®.

T-012

Der Name steht nicht nur als Synonym für die Adresse des Clubs, sondern verweist auf den berühmten Namensgeber: Theodor Heuss, erster deutscher Bundespräsident und Bürger von Stuttgart. Um ihm zu huldigen wurde eine Auswahl seiner berühmten Zitate, die ihn als Lebemann und Genussmenschen mit feinem Humor ausweisen, an die Wände entlang der Treppe angebracht. Alle Räume sind durchgehend in Schwarz und Weiß gehalten. Spiegel und groß-flächige Illustrationen verstärken den Raumeindruck. Die Fenster-front im Erdgeschoss ist mit einer Polarisationsfolie beklebt und zeigt bei Tageslicht eine Stadt-silhouette als verspiegelte Fläche. Abends, wenn der Club innen erleuchtet ist, löst sich das Motiv auf und gibt den Blick frei auf die freistehende, U-förmige Theke aus weißem Mineralwerkstoff.

T-012

Le nom n'est pas seulement celui du night-club, mais évoque égale-ment un grand homme : Theodor Heuss, premier président de la République fédérale d'Allemagne et citoyen de la ville de Stuttgart. Pour lui rendre hommage, un choix de citations qui mettent l'accent sur le politicien bon vivant à l'humour raffiné décore les murs de l'escalier. Toutes les salles sont en noir et blanc. Des miroirs et de grandes illustrations renforcent l'impression d'immen-sité de l'espace. Un film polariseur est collé sur les baies vitrées du rez-de-chaussée. À la lumière du jour, il réfléchit la silhouette d'un paysage urbain. Le soir, lorsque le club est éclairé de l'intérieur, le motif se dissout et on peut voir le comptoir en forme de U réalisé à partir d'un matériau minéral.

The wall behind the bar is roughly paneled in black-stained, brushed wood painted with oversized, white illustrations.

Hinter der Bar befindet sich eine grobe Wandverschalung aus gebürstetem, schwarz gebeiztem Holz, auf die großflächige Illustrationen gemalt sind.

Derrière le bar, un revêtement mural de bois brossé teint en noir est décoré de vastes illustrations.

The motifs are surrealistic adaptations of urban themes, enhanced by the placement of real objects, like a streetlamp, in a room.

Die Motive sind surreale Adaptionen urbaner Themen, die im Raum durch reale Objekte, wie etwa eine Straßenlampe, fortgesetzt werden.

Les motifs reprennent des thèmes urbains en les adaptant de manière quelque peu suréelle. Des objets bien réels, tel un lampadaire, viennent compléter cet univers.

Eastpak@Breuniger

The jazzunique team designed an impressive exhibition and sales area for the Eastpak brand. Best known for their handbags and backpacks, the area was designed to showcase their new apparel collection. The Eastpak area was designed to stand out from other nearby installations, inviting one into the "World of Eastpak." A cleverly thought out succession of contorted pink and black stripes covers the entire floor and walls of the exhibition area, running up the sides of the display fixtures to the top. The design spatially and visually communicates the progressive image of the fashion label.

Eastpak@Breuniger

Das Team von jazzunique entwarf eine beeindruckende Ausstellungs- und Verkaufsfläche für die Marke Eastpak, bekannt für ihre angesagten Taschen und Rucksäcke, die auf dieser Fläche insbesondere ihre neue Apparell Kollektion präsentierte. Die Fläche stach auffallend aus den umliegenden Installationen heraus und lud dazu ein, die "Eastpak Welt" zu entdecken. Eine ausgeklügelte Abfolge und Verzerrung von Streifen in pink und schwarz bedecken den gesamten Boden samt Wänden der Ausstellungsfläche und laufen an den Einbauten hoch. Räumlich als auch kommunikativ unterstützte die Fläche das progressive Image des Modelabels.

Eastpak@Breuniger

L'équipe de jazzunique a réalisé un espace d'exposition et de vente pour la marque Eastpak, spécialisée dans les sacs et sacs à dos. Cet espace hors du commun a servi de cadre à la présentation de la nouvelle collection de la marque, *Apparel*. Se démarquant de toutes les autres installations alentour, le stand invite à découvrir les produits de « l'univers Eastpak ». Un motif composé de raies roses et noires, dont la largeur peut varier tel un effet de déformation, recouvre le sol, les parois et les éléments d'équipement du stand. En termes de communication et d'agencement de l'espace, le stand s'accorde parfaitement avec l'image très moderne de ce label de mode.

Maverick Showroom

A space of only 80 sq feet/24 sq m had to be transformed into a prestige show room. Required were a high quality, image appropriate display space for the Maverick brand as well as an effective, usable workroom for sales talks and collection presentations. The idea was to take the pre-existing Maverick image and transform it, using simple materials, into a new graphic and spatial aesthetic. Brown packing tape cut to different sizes was stuck on the walls running this way and that, creating a completely new look. White graphics embodying the image of a stylish, unconventional fashion label worked like paper cut outs against the brown tape background. Shelves made of white pressboard were combined with steel piping into an intelligent, yet edgy, display system.

Maverick Showroom

Ein nur 24 m² großer Raum sollte in einen repräsentativen Showroom verwandelt werden. Gefragt waren eine hochwertige und imagegerechte Präsentation der Marke Maverick sowie ein effektiv nutzbarer Arbeitsraum für Verkaufsgespräche und Kollektionspräsentationen. Die Idee war, dass vorhandene Image der Marke Maverick mit einfachen Mitteln in einer neuen grafischen und räumlichen Ästhetik zu transportieren. Unterschiedlich lange Stücke handelsüblicher brauner Packbänder wurden kreuz und quer auf die Wände verklebt und ergeben so ein völlig neues Bild. Weiße Grafiken, die das Image eines stylischen, unkonventionellen Labels verkörpern, wirken wie ausgeschnitten. Regale aus weißen Pressspanplatten wurden mit Stahlrohren zu einem intelligenten und ungewöhnlichen Präsentationssystem kombiniert.

Showroom Maverick

Il s'agissait ici de transformer un modeste espace de 24 m² en un showroom représentatif du label. Le cahier des charges comprenait la réalisation d'un décor haut de gamme, à l'image de la marque Maverick, ainsi que l'agencement ingénieux d'un espace de travail servant à la fois de cadre pour les entretiens de vente et pour la présentation des collections. La gageure était de transcrire par des moyens simples l'image du label tant dans le graphisme que dans l'organisation de l'espace. On a coupé différentes longueurs d'un ruban adhésif d'emballage. Ces morceaux ont été ensuite collés au mur pour former des motifs géométriques. Les éléments graphiques blancs, qui incarnent l'image d'un label au style avant-gardiste, ressemblent à des papiers découpés. Les étagères en contre-plaqué blanc supportées par des tubes en acier constituent un système de rangement aussi original qu'ingénieux.

The simple furniture is graphically refined with flowery, Japanese-like patterns. The pattern was first cut into plastic film, which then served as a stencil for the paintings on the cubes.

Die einfachen Möbel wurden grafisch mit blumigen, japanisch anmutenden Mustern verfeinert. Die Muster wurden zuerst aus Folien ausgeschnitten, welche dann als Schablone für die Bemalung der „Cubes" dienten.

De forme très sobre, le mobilier est décoré de motifs floraux japonisants. Les motifs ont d'abord été découpés dans des feuilles de film plastique qui ont ensuite servi de pochoir pour peindre les cubes.

Joseph Kosuth

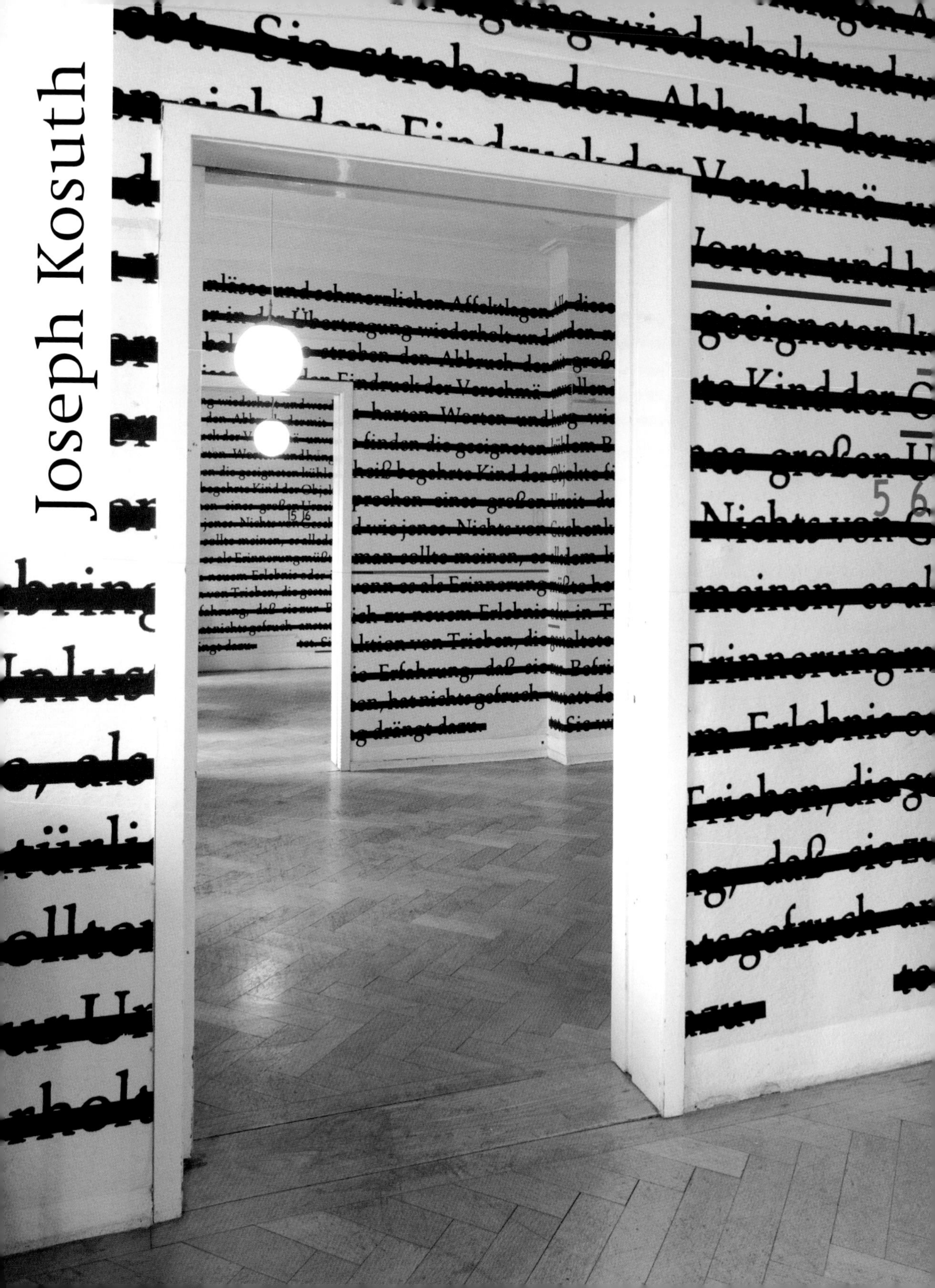

Zero & Not Installation

The American conceptual artist Joseph Kosuth lives in New York City, teaching, since 1968, in the School of Visual Arts (SVA). His installation Zero & Not took up the three exhibition rooms of the Galerie Kubinski in Stuttgart. He covered the walls with wallpaper. A quote from Sigmund Freud's Beyond the Pleasure Principle was mechanically printed on the wallpaper and repeated 15½ times throughout the rooms. The words were then partially crossed out, making them difficult to read. Due to the architecture of the gallery rooms, no text was written over doors and windows. The human eye, accustomed to written language, completes the entire text.

Zero & Not Installation

Der amerikanische Konzeptkünstler Joseph Kosuth lebt in New York und lehrt dort seit 1968 an der School for Visual Arts. Für seine Arbeit Zero & Not beschlagnahmte er alle drei Ausstellungsräume der damaligen Galerie Kubinski in Stuttgart, bzw. deren Wände die er mit der Tapete beklebte. Tapeziert ist ein Textabsatz aus „Jenseits des Lustprinzips" von Sigmund Freud, der sich 15½ Mal über die Räume wiederholt. Der Text ist durchgestrichen und nicht zum Lesen bestimmt. Bedingt durch die Architektur der Galerie wurde über Türen und Fenster kein Text aufgebracht. Das menschliche Auge, vertraut im Umgang mit geschriebener Sprache, vervollständigt den gesamten Text.

Installation *Zero & Not*

L'artiste conceptuel américain Joseph Kosuth vit à New York où il enseigne depuis 1968 à la School for Visual Arts. Pour son ouvrage *Zero & Not*, il a utilisé les trois salles d'exposition de l'ancienne galerie Kubinski à Stuttgart et plus précisément ses murs qu'il a tapissés de papiers peints. Le motif reprend un paragraphe du livre de Sigmund Freud, *Au-delà du principe de plaisir,* que l'on retrouve 15½ fois dans les salles. Le texte barré n'est en fait pas destiné à être lu. L'architecture du lieu reprend cet effet puisque dans les ouvertures que forment les portes et les fenêtres, le texte n'existe que dans la pensée. Toutefois, l'œil humain habitué à l'écriture, peut compléter le texte en son entier.

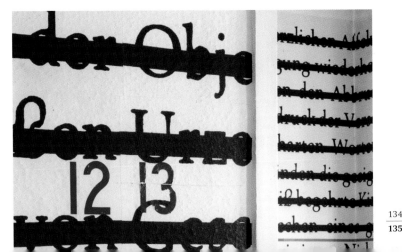

Wallpaper art walks the fine line between art for art's sake, ironic provocation and pleasing decoration. Frequently, an extraordinary idea or unusual combination of materials provides the impetus.

Tapetenkunst ist eine Gradwanderung zwischen künstlerischem Selbstzweck, ironischer Provokation und gefälliger Dekoration.
Oft ist es nur eine außergewöhnliche Idee oder eine ungewöhnliche Materialkombination die den Anstoß gibt.

L'art de la tapisserie oscille entre l'expression artistique, la provocation ironique et la fonction décorative. Souvent, une idée extravagante ou une association inhabituelle de matériaux sont à la base de la création d'un papier peint inédit.

L2M3 Kommunikationsdesign

Amsel
Turdus merula

Grünfink
Carduelis chloris

Kohlmeise
Parus major

Kreisparkasse Tübingen

The designs of the L2M3 agency bring a little bit of nature indoors. The silhouette of a tree, at a scale of 1:1, enlivens the concrete walls of the main stairway. The "flying objects" visible between the tree branches tell the visitor what floor he or she is approaching. These pictogram-like elements are not just stuck on the stairway walls near the tree, but wander throughout the entire building. Since the building itself is not open to the public and already very clearly laid out, the need to guide visitors through the building was not a top priority. This gave the designers a free hand. As a result, the guidance system has more of an ornamental character, lending a playful air to the severe, straightforward architecture, thus serving the reputation and building the image of the savings bank.

Kreissparkasse Tübingen

Die Gestaltung der Agentur L2M3 holt ein Stück Natur ins Haus. Der Schattenriss eines Baumes, im Maßstab 1:1 auf den Beton appliziert, belebt die Wände im Haupttreppenhaus. Verschiedene „Flugobjekte" rund um den Baum zeigen an, in welchem Stockwerk man sich befindet. Diese Piktogramm ähnlichen Elemente verharren nicht nur in der Nähe des Baumes im Treppenhaus, sondern wandern jeweils durch das ganze Stockwerk. Da der Bau selbst bereits sehr übersichtlich ist und da in einem nicht-öffentlichen Gebäude die Besucherführung nicht die zentrale Rolle spielt, war ein etwas freierer Umgang mit dem Leitsystem möglich. Es hat daher durchaus ornamentalen Charakter, bringt ein spielerisches Moment in die strenge, klare Architektur und dient der Repräsentation und Imagebildung für die Sparkasse.

Caisse d'épargne de Tübingen

La réalisation de l'agence L2M3 apporte un peu de nature dans cet espace. La silhouette d'un arbre grandeur nature appliquée sur du béton décore les parois de l'escalier principal. Autour de cet arbre sont disposés des éléments qui varient en fonction de l'étage où l'on se trouve. Ces éléments similaires à des pictogrammes ne se trouvent pas seulement près de l'arbre dans la cage d'escalier, mais sont disposés sur tout l'étage. Dans le contexte d'une architecture déjà très dépouillée et d'un immeuble fermé au public, donc sans nécessité d'indications pour les visiteurs, il a été possible de prendre davantage de liberté avec la décoration d'ensemble. Elle présente ainsi un caractère très ornemental, apporte une note ludique à l'architecture plutôt sévère et est également représentative de l'image que souhaite donner cet établissement.

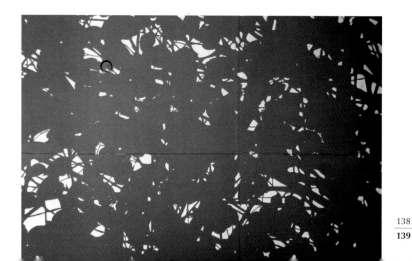

All the way at the top, children's kites seem to fly over the walls. One floor below, the flying objects are birds.

Ganz oben scheinen Kinderdrachen über die Wände zu fliegen, ein Geschoss tiefer sind es Vögel.

Tout en haut, des cerfs-volants d'enfants semblent voltiger sur les murs ; un étage en dessous, ce sont des oiseaux qui volent.

The next level below has butterflies, and the next, insects, followed at the bottom by falling leaves.

In der Etage darunter Schmetterlinge, dann andere Insekten, gefolgt von fallendem Laub.

En descendant, on voit des papillons, puis d'autres insectes, et plus bas des feuilles qui tombent.

M. Laussegger & E. Beierheimer

enpool identifikation
aginar imaginärer raum
ndividualtradition indivi
agestellung in frage stel
situ inspirieren installat
gration integrieren inte
splay interaktivitätskon
kompetenz interkulture
intervenionistische kuns
rritieren irritiert irritiert
katastrophale intelligent
e koexistenz koexistier
ntieren kommerzialisier
unikativer raum kommi
mpositionsmaterial kom
eigenschaft von sprach
tion von geschlecht kon
spezifisch kontextspezi
rter konvertieren konv
nstlerische auffassung
insatz körperlich körpe
ische kultur- und medie
turelle praxis.. kulturelle
g kulturverständnis kur
n kunstform kunstform
ktion künstlerischer ans
stem kunstszene kunst
g legitimieren legitim le
der beliebigkeit machtve
massenmedium massen
ren medial mediale rea
mehrdeutig mehrfach
isch minimal missachte
chrom monotonie mono
king museum museal n
etzwerk netzwerkartig n
chnologien neuordnung
nsichtlich offensive kon
nipotent online ontolo
n oszillierend output pa
aß partieren partiell pa
n performance perform
ologisch piktographisch
larisieren politisch polit
tentiell potenzieren pra
rezios primär prinzip p
atte profan programm
rotestieren protokollier
publizieren publikation
rationalisieren rational
äumliche verortung rau
uzieren reduziert refere
levanz relevant renom
t requisiten resistent
rhythmus rhythmisieren
ten schlüsselbegriff sch
ch selbstreflektiv selbstreflex
sequenzieren sequenziel
ität sinnambivalenz und bede
stisch soundart soundregie
kulativ spezialisiertes publiku
metrisch stereotyp stilisieren
zug subjektiv subjektive dim
sublimieren sublim suggerie
ntax synthese synthetisch

Words

In many cases, art today lives by means of its description in text form. In the process, the kinds of words used drown the art itself in an overwhelming construct of highly specialized vocabulary. Art is, as it were, given form by means of language. An ever-increasing number of technical terms and keywords buzz through the art world, a veritable deluge of language. It is in this context that the project Words came into being in 2004. The project is a collection of over 2500 terms, consisting of a total of 3500 individual words. The list of these textual building blocks is continually brought up to date and expanded. Since 2005 a number of different works have been produced using Words—including wallpaper.

Worte

In vielen Fällen lebt die Kunst heutzutage von ihrer textlichen Beschreibung. Dabei wird die Formensprache der Kunst oft durch ein übermächtiges Konstrukt an hoch spezialisiertem Vokabular übertönt. Das Kunstwerk wird sozusagen erst mit dem Werkzeug Sprache in Form gebracht. Eine ständig wachsende Vielzahl solcher „Fachwörter" bzw. „Keywords" schwirrt durch die Kunstwelt und erzeugt eine sprachliche Reizüberflutung. In diesem Sinn entstand seit 2004 das Projekt „WORTE", einer Sammlung aus über 2500 Begriffen, die wiederum aus ca. 3500 Wörtern bestehen. Diese Liste von Textbausteinen wird ständig aktualisiert und erweitert. Seit 2005 entstanden verschiedene Arbeiten – wie z.B. Tapeten – mit diesen „Worten".

Les mots

Dans de nombreux cas, l'art vit aujourd'hui de sa description par le texte. Le langage de l'art se dissimule souvent derrière des notions très élaborées. Pour ainsi dire, l'œuvre d'art n'acquiert sa forme qu'avec l'outil « langue ». Un nombre sans cesse croissant de termes techniques ou *keywords* a envahi le domaine de l'art et engendre une véritable exaspération linguistique. C'est ainsi qu'est né en 2004 le projet WORTE (mots), une collection de plus de 2 500 notions, réunissant quelque 3 500 mots. Cette liste de termes est continuellement actualisée et élargie. Depuis 2005, divers travaux, dont des papiers peints ont pris ces « mots » pour motif.

entwicklern etymologie produktionsprozess realität form freiraum generativ gesellschaft gruppieren illu
logexpansive peripherie form freiraum gedanken generativ gesellschaft gliedern hybride objekte illt
v feminismus formalisierbar kuratorisch gedächtnis gestaltetik form aufbrechen gliedern hybride illuminieren improvis
alismus formell/kuratorisch gedächtnis gestästhetik form aufbrechen gliedern grundmotiv arbeiten illuminieren inform
dimenthaft freie/kuratorische form gegenwartskunst gestaltetik form gliederung grundmotiv herausarbeiten illuminieren kompensatio
d gastkuratorische gegenwartskunst geschlossene form gliederung grundmotiv herausarbeiten improvisieren informationsschicht kompensatio
rtspezifisch geschlechtergerecht grundlegend hegemonial hybrid hybriden improvisieren informationsschicht kompensa
rchtsbestätigung gleichlage grundlegend hegemonial hybrid hybridbildung konzentrieren inkompetenz interaktiv inter
gerechtigung selbstdarstellung horror vacui ideologie ignorieren improvisation inkompetenz interagieren interface interf
e verzerrung horizontalpolitik impressum informationen inklusiv instrumentalisieren interagieren interface interf
hedonistische horizontalpolitik impressum informationen inklusiv instrumentalisieren interagieren interpretationspostulat involvie
homogen identifikation implizit impressum informationen inkludieren instrument interaktion interpretationspostulat kapitel
klimakrise identifikation implizieren intiier intention interaktion interessensfeld interpretationspostulat kla
tion impliziten informations/in intier instrument intention interaktion interpretation invertieren machtmittel kla
striell informationsinitiator/in intensiv öffentlichkeit intention inversion invertieren machtmittel kleinformatig geda
initiative rahmen institutionen intensiv öffentlichkeit interpretationsmodell inversion invertieren kollektives geda
ller rahmen intensivieren intensive interpretationsparameter kapitalistisch klappentext kollektiv komm
sität intensivieren interessierte geschichte interpretationsparameter kapitalistisch klappentext komplizenschaft kons
n interpretiert geschichte inventarisiert kapital kapitalistische klangsynthese kollidieren kommunikationsnetzwerk konfrontativ
alkulieren kalkuliert kapital kapitalistisch klangsynthese autorenschaft kommunikationsmöglichkeit konfrontieren konspirativ kontext ki
klangarchitektur kollektiv klangstruktur kollektive audiovisuelle kommunikationsmöglichkeit kontemporär kontext kor
ktionsform kollektiv kommunikationsform komplexe audiovisuelle konfrontation kontemplativ kontur konzeptionell konz
unikationsform komplex komplexe konflikt konform konservieren kontemplativ kontur konzeption konzeptsystem kunst kor
komplexität konflikt konsequent kontemplieren kontemplativ kontrovers kontur konzeption konzeptsystem kunst kreolisierung akt
eren konferieren konsequenz kontemplation kontrastreich kontrovers konzeptuell kreieren kreolisierung kulturelle akt
ks konsequenz kontemplation kontrastieren kontextuell konzeptueller koordinaten kreieren kreolisierung kulturelle kun
ntaktnetz kontemplation konzeptualisieren koordinate kreativer ansatz kulturelle kodierung diskurs kulturelle kun
nkei konzept konzeptualisieren kooperieren kreativer ansatz kulturelle kulturpolitischer diskurs kunstaktion kun
ate kooperation korrespondierend kulturprogramm kulturpolitisch und diskussion kunstinnenvereinigung kun
rrespondieren kulturaustausch kulturpolitisch kunst und diskussion kunstinnenvereinigung kun
rre kulturarbeit kulturkritisch im kontext kunst und kunstlerinnen kunstmultiplikator kunstobj
ulturkonsument kulturschaffende kunst im kontext kunstlerinnenprojekt kunstmultiplikator kunstmultiplikator lapidar lectu
und kulturschaffende kulturschaffende kunst kunstlerinnenprojekt kunstmaschine kunstmultiplikator langfristig lokale struktu
kunstlerinnenorganisation kunstmarkt kunstmaschine landscape lokale formen lokale struktu
rstandnis künstlich labor labyrinth lakonisch lokal beschränkt lokale orte markant markierung markieren
bernetik label logo lokal labyrinth lokal beschränkt lokale orte markant mechanisch mechanische
logistik logo lokal marginal marginale mechanismus mechanisieren mechanisch medienreflexiv
anovrieren manuell manuell mechanisch medienproduktion medienreflexivität migration
kunst matrix mazen/in mechanisch medienproduktion medienreflexivität metier metonymisch modul modulh
kunst medienlandschaft der kunstbetrachtung modifikation metier metonymisch modul modul
methodisch methoden der kunstbetrachtung modifizieren multimedia-performance eler
modellhaft modellhafte darstellung multimediabaukasten navigieren narratives eler
motiv motivation multimedia narrativ narrative formen neu interpretieren neuanordnung
nachtrag namedropping narrativ neuinterpretation neu interpretieren objekthaft objektbegriff ob
ulierung neu normieren neuinterpretation objekt objekthaft objektbegriff öffentlichke
 formativ nuance oberfläche oberflächlich objekt objekthaft öffentlicher raum öffentlichkeit öffentlichke
er diskurs öffentlicher freiraum öffentlicher raum ort der produktion ortsbezo
ental ort ort der produktion ort der erinnerung ort der produktion parameter parametrisier
enwechsel paradoxon paradox parallelen parallel parameter peinture pend
lekte passage passieren pastellmild patchwork pedantisch persistenz persistieren perspe
manent permutieren persiflage persiflieren persistenz plattform plattform für den üb
ungsprozess plastisch plastische intervention plattform position positionieren
kulturelle gesellschaften poros, portabel portfolio position positionieren präskribieren
entationsplattform präsenz präsent präsente unmittelbarkeit präskribieren
atisch produktion produzieren produktiv produktionskosten produktionsm
ression project in progress projekt projektieren projektion projizieren proj
zess prozesshaft prozessual prozessuale strukturen pseudo-realistisch psy
einschnitte radikale konsequenz radikale provokation rahmen randbereich
tion raumkontraktion räumlich räumliche abfolge räumliche bezüge räumli
tiv realisation realisieren real real virtuality realisierungsmöglichkeit realis
ung rekapitulieren rekonstruktion rekonstruieren rekonstruktion von wirklic
umieren retrospektiv revidieren rezeption rezipieren rezeptionsorientierte
n sarkastisch schablone schablonieren schablonenhaft schaffensprozess
emantisch semiologisch semiotik semiotisch semipermeabilität semiperma
ieren signifikant signifie signifikativ simplifikation simplifizieren simulatio
n situiert skeptisch skills skizzieren skulptur skulpturen skulptur skul
es beobachten soziokulturell soziolekt spannungsfeld spannungslinie spa
kturieren strukturell strukturelle beschaffenheit struktureller umbruch strukt
h symbolträchtig subphänomen subroutine substitution substituieren
erial textsynthese taktil tangente symmetrie symmetrisch symptomatisch synchron syne
bildung theoriefixiert theoriekonstrukt theorierelevant these tape tapen tätigkeitsfeld ti
transformationell transformativ transformativer akt transitiv these thematisch top
scht umschreibend überflüssig transformation überformung transitiv überfrachten top
ben umschreibend unzureichend umsetzen umweg überformen überfrachten
träger verbalisieren unzureichend unzureichende undifferenziert uneinde
en verkörpern vermeidung einfacher verbinden verbindendes thematisierung über
versuch versuchen versuchsweise auskunfte verbindendes element update und
vielschichtiges spektrum virtual reality versus vertikal verweigern verdichtung
kabular vordergrundig vor-ort-diskussion virtuell virtuelle ausstellung verwickeln
iterentwickeln werkstatt wettbewerb white cube wahrnehmung wahrnehmen virtue
produktion werkstatt wettbewerb white cube wahrnehmung wahrnehmen wah
d zielgruppe zielsetzung zeichen zeichenvokabular widerspruch wider
den zweideutig zweidimensional zirkulieren zirkular zitat zeichnen zitat
zweidimensional zweidimensional

marburg wallcoverings

Wallpapers and art

The Marburg wallpaper factory has been in existence for 160 years. Johann Bertram Schaefer founded it in 1845 as a shop specializing in interior furnishings. Since then, over four generations, the firm has developed into one of the leading wallpaper manufacturers in the world. The house collections are diverse and divided into categories: Modern, Classic, Romantic and Opulent. But marburg wallcoverings are not only dependent on its own designs when it comes to keeping its finger on the pulse of the times. For many years, the firm has worked closely together with a variety of designers and artists. Whether it is the calm geometric patterns and color lines created by the artist Richard Anuszkiewicz, or the sensual minimalism of a Karim Rashid, the wallpapers produced by the factory in Marburg are always distinctive.

Tapeten und Kunst

Die Marburger Tapetenfabrik besteht bereits seit 160 Jahren. Angefangen hatte alles 1845 – da eröffnete Johann Bertram Schaefer in Marburg ein Fachgeschäft für Innenausstattung. Seitdem hat sich das Unternehmen, durch vier Generationen hindurch, zu einem der führenden Tapetenhersteller gewandelt. Die Kollektionen des Hauses sind vielfältig und teilen sich in vier Kategorien: Modern, Klassik, Romantik und Opulenz. Aber nicht nur mit den eigenen Dessins sind die Marburger Tapetenfabrikanten am Puls der Zeit. Seit vielen Jahren arbeitet das Unternehmen mit verschiedenen Designern und Künstlern eng zusammen. Ob sensibel geometrische Kunstmotive und Farbverläufe, basierend auf Originalwerken des Künstlers Richard Anuszkiewicz, oder sinnlicher Minimalismus eines Karim Rashid: die Tapeten der Marburger Fabrik sind unverwechselbar.

Papiers peints et art

La manufacture de tapisserie de Marburg existe depuis 160 ans déjà. Tout a commencé en 1845, lorsque Johann Bertram Schaefer ouvrit à Marburg un magasin spécialisé en architecture d'intérieur. Au fil du temps, l'entreprise a traversé cinq générations pour devenir un des fabricants allemands leaders en tapisserie. Très diversifiées, les collections de la maison se divisent en quatre catégories : moderne, classique, romantique et opulente. Mais les fabricants de Marburg ne sont pas seulement à la pointe du progrès avec leurs propres créations. Depuis de nombreuses années, ils travaillent en étroite collaboration avec divers designers et artistes. Que ce soit les délicats motifs géométriques et les coulées de couleurs extraites d'œuvres de l'artiste Richard Anuszkiewicz, ou le minimalisme sensuel de Karim Rashid, les papiers peints de la manufacture de Marburg sont uniques en leur genre.

In 2005, Werner Berges, a beloved figure in the German world of Pop Art, designed a very special collection.

2005 entstand mit einem der bedeutendsten deutschen Vertreter der Pop Art, Werner Berges, eine ganz besondere Kollektion.

En 2005, une collection très originale a été créée en collaboration avec Werner Berges, un des principaux représentants de l'art Pop en Allemagne.

As with his pictures, his wallpaper themes are glamour, seduction, beauty and eroticism.

Die Themen seiner Bilder und somit auch seiner Tapetenmuster sind Glanz, Verführung, Schönheit und Erotik.

Éclat, séduction, beauté et érotisme sont les thèmes des œuvres que l'on retrouve dans ses papiers peints.

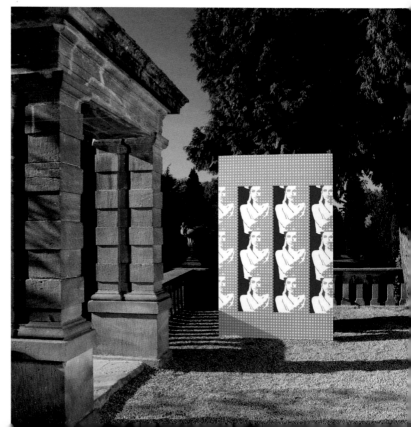

Ingo Maurer

LED Wall Panels

Ingo Maurer, the old master of lighting design, uniquely combines design and technology to produce amazing, poetic effects. His lighting objects have stories to tell, fantastic, always surprising, exciting stories. Maurer's work articulates his strong interest employing technological innovation in a search for new aesthetic and decorative solutions. His current project is the design of LED wall panels—essentially wallpaper equipped with light-emitting electronic diodes. The illumination creates a perceptual experience that is both extraordinary and visually confusing in a thought-provoking way. We have always associated light with three-dimensional fixtures. By breaking this convention, Ingo Maurer has made the association two-dimensional. In the process, the light becomes architectural, a wall unto itself.

LED-Wandpaneel

Der Altmeister des Lichts, Ingo Maurer, vereint in seiner Tapete Design und Technologie auf eine einzigartige Weise und bringt dabei immer wieder verblüffende und poetische Effekte hervor. Seine Lichtobjekte erzählen Geschichten – voller Phantasie, immer überraschend und spannend. In seinen Arbeiten artikuliert sich eine starke Faszination an technischen Innovationen und ein Interesse, diese zu neuen ästhetischen und dekorativen Lösungen zu führen. Sein aktuelles Projekt, das LED-Wandpaneel, eine mit Leuchtdioden bestückte Tapete, erzeugt ein Wahrnehmungserlebnis, das außergewöhnlich und irritierend zugleich ist. Bislang verband man mit dekorativem Licht dreidimensionale Lichtobjekte, Ingo Maurer bricht mit diesem Prinzip und überführt es in die Zweidimensionalität. Das Licht wird Teil der Architektur, es wird selbst zur Wand.

Panneau mural LED

Maître de la lumière, Ingo Maurer réunit brillamment design et technologie dans ses papiers peints avec à chaque fois de stupéfiants effets poétiques. Ses « objets lumineux » racontent des histoires pleines de fantaisie, toujours étonnantes et excitantes. Dans ses travaux, une énorme fascination pour les innovations techniques s'associe à une recherche incessante de nouvelles solutions décoratives et esthétiques. Son projet actuel, le panneau mural LED, une tapisserie dotée de diodes, intrigue et captive l'attention de l'observateur. Jusqu'à présent, la lumière décorative a toujours été associée aux objets lumineux tridimensionnels ; Ingo Maurer rompt avec ce principe qu'il projette dans le bidimensionnel. La lumière s'intègre dans l'architecture en devenant elle-même un mur.

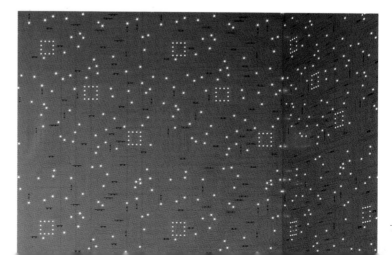

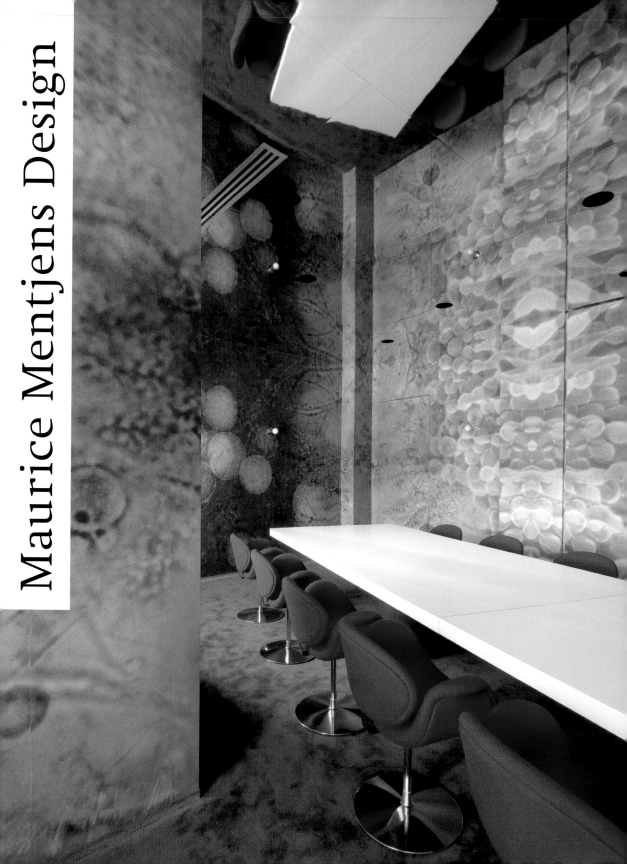

Maurice Mentjens Design

DSM Headquarters

This conference room needs to represent the firm as well as fulfill a variety of functions. Dinner can be served there for two or 20 people, or even up to 30 on festive occasions. The walls of the room are covered with large format panoramic images appropriate to this pharmaceutical and chemical company's new field of activity: biotechnology. Mentjens decided on a dominant motif of using images of the microscopic world of enzymes and bacteria as wallcoverings. Using graphic design software, the photographs were altered so as to produce an abstract, seemingly psychedelic representation.

DSM Headquarters

Der Konferenzraum sollte repräsentative ebenso wie funktionale Funktionen übernehmen: Dinner oder Meetings für zwei bis 20 Personen oder kurze festliche Anlässe mit bis zu dreißig Personen. Die Wände des Zimmers wurden mit großformatigen Panoramabildern bedeckt. Passend zum neuen Tätigkeitsfeld des Unternehmens, einer biotechnologischen Abteilung, entschied sich Mentjens die Fotografie einer mikroskopisch kleinen Welt, bestehend aus Enzymen und Bakterien, als Wandverkleidung einzusetzen. Mithilfe einer Grafiksoftware wurde das Bild so bearbeitet, dass eine abstrakte, psychedelisch anmutende Darstellung entstand.

DSM Headquarters

La salle de conférence de la société DSM devait être représentative et fonctionnelle puisqu'elle était également destinée à servir de salle à manger pouvant accueillir jusqu'à vingt personnes, ou de salle de réception pour une trentaine de personnes. Les murs de la salle ont été recouverts de panneaux panoramiques grand format. S'inspirant du nouveau secteur d'activités de l'entreprise, un service de biotechnologie, Maurice Mentjens a choisi la reproduction d'un univers microscopique d'enzymes et de bactéries comme motif du revêtement mural. Avec l'aide d'un logiciel graphique, la photographie a été travaillée jusqu'à l'obtention d'une image abstraite, de facture psychédélique.

Café Ipanema

The restaurant, designed in part by the famous architect Aldo Rossi, includes subtle designer furniture and one-of-a-kind productions. There are tables with brick legs supporting heavy wooden tabletops, but also lightweight plastic tables and chairs by the English designer Jasper Morrison. The element of restraint brings out the formal design aspects exceptionally well. Colored Plexiglas windows filter light into the room, creating unusual effects. The walls are a particular highlight, with different wallpapers applied as collage. Seemingly traditional patterns in discreet colors overlap with dazzlingly modern decor.

Café Ipanema

Die Einrichtung, zum Teil ebenfalls von Aldo Rossi entworfen, wurde durch unaufdringliche Designermöbel und spezielle Anfertigungen ergänzt. Es finden sich Tische mit Füßen aus Backsteinen und schweren Holzplatten, ebenso wie leichte Kunststofftische und -stühle des englischen Designers Jasper Morrison. Diese Zurückhaltung bringt die weiteren gestalterischen Elemente besonders gut zur Geltung. Durch farbige Plexiglasscheiben an den Fenstern wird das Licht gefiltert und ungewöhnliche Lichteffekte erzielt. Besonderes Highlight sind aber die Wände. Wie eine Collage sind verschiedene Tapeten an die Wand geklebt. Traditionell anmutende Muster in dezenten Farben überlappen sich mit modernen, grellen Dekoren.

Café Ipanema

Cet espace, conçu en partie par Aldo Rossi, est doté d' un mobilier au design sobre et d'éléments réalisés spécialement pour ce lieu. On y trouve des tables aux lourds plateaux de bois reposant sur des pieds en briques, mais aussi des tables et des chaises légères en matière plastique du designer anglais Jasper Morrison. Cette sobriété rehausse l'effet des autres éléments de décoration. Les vitres de Plexiglas légèrement colorées filtrent la lumière, produisant des reflets lumineux insolites. Mais le clou de l'aménagement intérieur se trouve sur les murs : divers papiers peints tapissent les parois à la manière d'un collage. Des motifs traditionnels aux coloris délicats chevauchent des motifs modernes aux couleurs vives pour former un décor d'une grande originalité.

Restaurant Witloof

This design is significantly influenced by Maurice Mentjens' interpretation of the typical Belgian interior. Toward this end, he employs a variety of wall and floor treatments that visually demarcate individual areas, giving each its own personality. The entryway resembles a log cabin in the Ardennes Forest. Shiny, white tiles define the next sector of the room. Dark green, Baroque-style wallpaper and stone flooring define the space in the rear. Neon tubes mark the border separating the entry area from the other rooms, symbolizing the line between the Flemish and Walloon provinces.

Restaurant Witloof

Seine eigene Interpretation eines, für Maurice Mentjens typischen belgischen Interieurs, setzte er in diesem Entwurf konsequent um. Als Stilmittel verwendet er dabei verschiedene Wand- und Bodenbeläge, die einzelne Bereiche zerschneiden und ihnen somit eine eigenständige Persönlichkeit geben. Der Eingangsbereich ähnelt einer Blockhütte in den Ardennen. Glänzende weiße Fliesen charakterisieren den nächsten Abschnitt. Im hinteren Bereich dominieren dunkelgrüne Barock-Tapeten und ein Steinboden. Die Trennung zwischen dem Eingangsbereich und den weiteren Räumen, wird durch eine rote Neonröhre markiert, diese steht für die Trennungslinie der Flämischen und Wallonischen Provinzen.

Restaurant Witloof

Dans le cadre de l'aménagement de ce restaurant, Maurice Mentjens a donné libre cours à sa vision d'un intérieur typiquement belge. Pour ce faire, il a utilisé divers revêtements de sols et de murs qui délimitent différents espaces et leur donnent chacun un cachet particulier. L'entrée ressemble à un chalet des Ardennes. Un carrelage d'un blanc brillant caractérise l'espace suivant. Du papier peint baroque vert foncé et un sol en pierre donnent son identité à l'arrière-salle du restaurant. Un tube de néon rouge sépare l'entrée des autres salles ; il symbolise également la frontière entre les provinces wallonnes et flamandes.

In the cellar, Neo-Baroque floral patterns are used against the dark tile of the walls, and reoccur as a motif on the black carpet.

Neo-Barocke Blumenmuster finden sich hier im Keller auf den dunklen Fliesen und als Motiv auf den schwarzen Tapeten.

Le même motif floral baroque se retrouve sur le papier peint et le carrelage sombres de la salle en sous-sol.

The impression on the visitor is that of a chapel or crypt of a church.

Der Besucher erhält den Eindruck sich in einer Kapelle oder Krypta zu befinden.

Le visiteur a l'impression de se trouver dans une chapelle ou dans une crypte.

Wallpaper projects

Natasha and Philipp Meuser work in collaboration with a team of architects at the interface between practice and theory. Their projects involve architecture, interior decoration and furniture design, as well as exhibition planning and publications on architecture and urbanism in an international context. As an example, the wallpaper here is based on an abstraction of a folk motif from Kazakhstan that the designers found on an old carpet. The designs are based on patterns and ornamentation reminiscent of grandmother's living room or one's own childhood bedroom.

Tapetenprojekte

Natascha und Philipp Meuser arbeiten gemeinsam mit einem Team aus Architekten und Redakteuren an der Schnittstelle zwischen Praxis und Theorie. Neben planerischen Aufgaben im Bereich Architektur, Innenarchitektur und Möbelentwurf befasst sich das Büro mit der Konzeption von Ausstellungen und Publikationen zu Architektur und Städtebau im internationalen Kontext. Bei der Gestaltung der folgenden Tapetenmotive ging es zum Beispiel um die Abstraktion von folkloristischen kasachischen Ornamenten, die in einem alten Teppich gefunden wurden. Die Entwürfe sind durch Muster und Ornamente beeinflusst, die man noch aus den Wohnzimmern seiner Großeltern oder aus dem eigenen Kinderzimmer her kennt.

Projets de tapisserie

Natascha et Philipp Meuser travaillent avec une équipe d'architectes et de rédacteurs au croisement de la théorie et de la pratique. Outre la planification de projets d'architecture, d'architecture d'intérieur et de conception de mobilier, les activités du bureau comprennent la réalisation d'expositions et de publications sur l'architecture et l'urbanisme dans un contexte international. Les motifs des papiers peints reproduits ici sont une reproduction abstraite d'ornements folkloriques kazakhs, découverts dans un tapis ancien. Les motifs et éléments de décoration que l'on peut encore voir dans le salon de ses grands-parents ou même dans son ancienne chambre d'enfant ont inspiré cette série de papiers peints contemporains.

This aerial photograph gives the applicant some idea of where he or she might soon be traveling.

Das Luftbild des Potsdamer Platzes lässt den Antragsteller erahnen, wohin er demnächst reisen wird.

La vue aérienne de la Potsdamer Platz à Berlin donne des idées de voyages.

The design communicates the image of modern Germany in the city formerly known as Königsberg.

Der Entwurf zielt auf die Vermittlung eines modernen Deutschland-Bildes im ehemaligen Königsberg.

Ce projet a pour objectif de présenter une image moderne de l'Allemagne à Kaliningrad.

The decor of the British embassy in Astana, Kazakhstan serves as a reference to the home country. At first, the image of the Union Jack distorted into 4 inch/10 cm rectilinear areas of color, is visually confusing, becoming clearer as the viewer moves further and further away.

Bei der Britischen Botschaft in Astana sollte ein Bezug zum Heimatland hergestellt werden. Die Auflösung des Union Jacks in etwa 10 cm große Punkte verursacht beim Betrachter zunächst eine Verwirrung. Erst aus einer Entfernung von etwa fünf Metern erschließt sich das Gesamtmotiv.

À l'ambassade britannique d'Astana, on souhaitait présenter une évocation de la patrie. L'image de l'Union Jack décomposée en gros points d'environ 10 cm désoriente d'abord l'observateur. Mais en s'éloignant de cinq mètres, on redécouvre le motif du célèbre drapeau.

Ulf Moritz

Although Ulf Moritz completed his first collection for the Marburg wallpaper factory in 2002, it remains relevant today. The discreet play of color and pattern set the tone for the bold, geometric formal language of the designer. Squares, rectangles and circles work together to form a harmonious pattern in the series Compendium, where an eastern clarity combines archaic forms and pure material effects into unique wallpaper. Moritz takes gray and silver base hues and enriches them with the addition of a chic violet. Special effects include metallic accents, coarse sand, fine creasing and flocking.

Die erste Kollektion von Ulf Moritz für die Marburger Tapetenfabrik stammt bereits aus dem Jahr 2002. Doch sie ist heute noch aktuell. Dezente Farbspiele und unaufdringliche Muster geben den Ton an. Der Designer wählte als Basis für seine Dessins eine strenge geometrische Formensprache: Quadrat, Rechteck und Kreis ergeben harmonische Muster. Zu dieser Reihe harmoniert die Kollektion Compendium hervorragend: Hier vereinen sich fernöstliche Klarheit mit archaischen Formen und puren Materialeffekten zu einer einzigartigen Tapete. Graue und silberne Basistöne kombiniert Moritz mit mondänem Violett. Hinzu kommen innovative Metallics, grobkörnige Sandeffekte, edle Knitterstrukturen und feine Effektvliese.

La première collection d'Ulf Moritz pour la manufacture de tapisserie de Marburg date de 2002. Mais elle n'a à ce jour rien perdu de son actualité. De discrètes nuances et des motifs sobres dominent dans cette série. Le designer a choisi un langage géométrique très concis de carrés, rectangles et cercles qui forment des motifs harmonieux. La collection compendium est fidèle à cette série. La clarté asiatique se marie à des formes archaïques et à la beauté primaire des matériaux pour créer un papier peint unique en son genre. Moritz associe des nuances basiques de gris et d'argent à un violet élégant. S'y ajoutent des métaux innovants, des effets de sable à gros grains, de sompteuses structures froissées et de délicats effets textiles.

The soft, expressive colors are rich and sensual. The designs are reminiscent of classic Baroque, Rococo and Japanese motifs.

Reich und sinnlich wirken die weichen, ausdrucksstarken Farben. Die Designs erinnern an klassische Barock- und Rokokosujets und japanische Reminiszenzen.

Les couleurs à la fois douces et fortes donnent une impression de richesse et de volupté. Les motifs rappellent les thèmes classiques du baroque ou du rococo, et ceux de l'art japonais ancien.

Adhesive stickers with naturalistic motifs also draw the eye.

Selbstklebende Sticker mit naturalistisch gezeichneten Motiven sind zusätzliche Blickfänger.

Des stickers autocollants représentant des motifs figuratifs parachèvent la décoration murale et retiennent l'attention.

The appearance of the Botanicus changes from matte to glossy depending on how the light falls.

Das Dekor Botanicus variiert in der Optik je nach Lichteinfall, von ganz matt bis glänzend.

Selon le degré de clarté dans la pièce, le décor *Botanicus* varie du mat au brillant.

The pure, structured Unis harmoniously unites a smaller leaf pattern with a decorative column of stylized Ginkgo branches.

Zu den puren, strukturierten Unis harmonisiert das reduzierte Blattmuster, eine dekorative Ranke stilisierter Ginkoblätter.

Le motif floral stylisé représentant des vrilles de feuilles de ginkgo s'harmonise admirablement à la pureté des unis structurés.

Motorberlin

Victoria Bar

The Victoria Bar is the very image of a bar as imagined by the designers of the Motorberlin agency. The design is a creative team project involving Georg Sagurna, Holger Kück, Ingo Strobel, C+M Architects and artist Thomas Hauser, and is stamped with the ideas of each participant. The patterned wallpaper was made by hand, with Stu Mead responsible for the walls of the rear corridor. Equal attention was given to each room to maintain a certain level of natural coherence, while allowing conscious breaks in the program as a means of keeping the visual excitement level high. Many details only become obvious after the third look—or third drink.

Victoria Bar

In der Victoria Bar kann das Bild einer Bar besichtigt werden, wie es sich die Designer der Agentur Motorberlin vorstellt. Das Projekt, eine Teamarbeit von Georg Sagurna, Holger Kück und Ingo Strobel mit den Architekten C+M und dem Künstler Thomas Hauser, ist geprägt durch eine Vielzahl von Impulsen aller Beteiligten. Die Tapeten mit Ihren Mustern wurden in Handarbeit hergestellt, für die Tapete im hinteren Flur zeichnet sich Stu Mead verantwortlich. Es wurde gleichermaßen auf gewisse Stimmigkeiten und Selbstverständlichkeiten geachtet, wie darauf, dass bewusste Brüche den Gesamteindruck lange spannend bleiben lassen. So findet man manches Detail erst nach dem dritten Hinsehen oder nach dem dritten Drink.

Victoria Bar

Le Victoria Bar est pour les designers de l'agence Motorberlin l'illustration même de la notion de bar. Ce travail d'équipe a réuni Georg Sagurna, Holger Kück, Ingo Strobel, les architectes de C+M et l'artiste Thomas Hauser. Le projet est donc soumis à des influences diverses. Les papiers peints et leurs motifs ont été fabriqués à la main. Les dessins de la tapisserie au fond du vestibule sont l'œuvre de l'artiste Stu Mead. La recherche d'une certaine unité et clarté dans l'aménagement a été un critère, de même que l'apport de ruptures délibérées afin de conserver une impression d'ensemble fascinante. C'est ainsi que certains détails ne se révèlent qu'après une observation minutieuse.

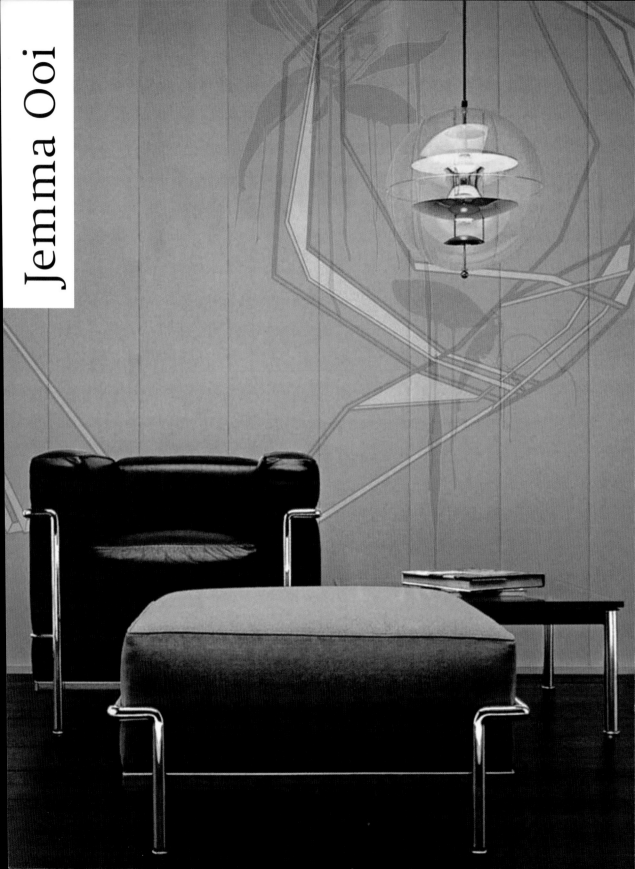

Jemma Ooi

Hybrid, Scratch, 26a

The English designer Jemma Ooi has garnered considerable attention for unique wallpaper designs that are like small-scale works of art, giving each room its own atmosphere. Her collages of human body parts interspersed with sketched elements create an exceptional image. Jemma Ooi's graphic style is multilayered, offering a completely different way of looking at walls. The viewer slowly comes to recognize the motif, citation, or face behind, between and underneath the linear foreground. The collections consist of wallpaper panels that can be combined to provide a variety of different wall treatments.

Hybrid, Scratch, 26a

Die englische Designerin Jemma Ooi sorgt mit ihren einzigartigen Tapetenmotiven für Aufmerksamkeit. Sie wirken wie kleine Kunstwerke und geben den Räumen einen ganz individuellen Charakter. Collagen aus Bildern von menschlichen Körperteilen mit handgezeichneten Skizzen erzeugen ein ungewöhnliches Bild. Ihre Grafiken sind vielschichtig und lassen immer wieder neue Betrachtungsweisen zu. Betrachter ihrer Kollektion erkennen Motive, Zitate, Gesichter hinter, zwischen und unter den linearen Strukturen. Ihre Kollektionen bestehen aus unterschiedlichen Paneelen, die sich zu vielfältigen Varianten untereinander kombinieren lassen.

Hybrid, Scratch, 26a

La créatrice anglaise Jemma Ooi s'est fait un nom avec des motifs hors norme. Ils ressemblent à de petites oeuvres d'art et confèrent à chaque espace un caractère très particulier. Des collages d'illustrations de parties du corps humain associés à des croquis dessinés à la main produisent un décor singulier. Complexes et stratifiés, les dessins dévoilent sans cesse de nouvelles perspectives. Un observateur attentif reconnaît des motifs, des citations, des visages derrière, entre et sous les structures linéaires. Les collections du designer se composent de différents éléments que l'on peut conjuguer en une multitude de variations.

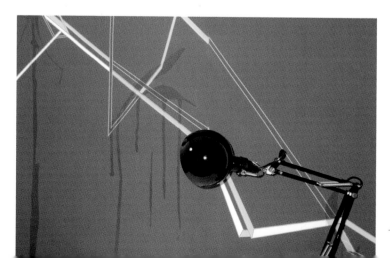

The Hybrid line explores the relationship between the human form and nature. The design 26a is a unique, hand-painted installation, a contiguous image drawn on the walls of three rooms of a house. There is only one place in the house from which the viewer can take in the entire drawing. From everywhere else, it just looks like an unusual pattern.

Die Verbindung der Bewegungen menschlicher Formen und der Natur ist Thema der Hybrid-Dekore. Bei 26a handelt es sich um eine spezielle, handgemalte Installation. Diese Grafik wurde durchgehend auf die Wände dreier Räume eines Hauses gezeichnet. Nur von einem Punkt des Hauses ist es dem Betrachter möglich, das gesamte Bild zu erfassen. Ansonsten wirken die Zeichnungen wie ungewöhnliche Muster.

Le mariage du mouvement humain et de la nature constitue le thème du décor *Hybrid*. *26a* est le nom d'une installation spéciale, peinte à la main. Le motif s'étend sur les murs de trois pièces. L'observateur ne peut découvrir l'image dans son ensemble que d'un seul endroit de la maison. Ses composants semblent en effet former des motifs séparés.

Jemma Ooi's wallpaper patterns are both subtle and intense, soft and loud, dreamy and insane.

Bei Jemma Ooi gibt es zurückhaltende, aufdringliche, leise, laute, verträumte und verrückte Tapetenmuster.

Jemma Ooi crée des motifs discrets, entêtants, délicats, éclatants, féeriques et extravagants.

This is art on the wall. Every design is an experience in color, shape and form.

Hier ist Kunst an der Wand. Jeder Entwurf wird zum Erlebnis in Form, Farbe und Gestalt.

De l'art sur les murs. Chaque ouvrage fascine par ses formes, ses couleurs et son contenu.

Interactive Wallpaper

In all of his work, Christopher Pearson incorporates architect Robert Venturi's theory of mediating space, understood as a zone for iconography and transmission of signs. Pearson took this idea a step further in his studies at the Royal College of Art, where he described the effect of different mediating influences on the formation of the urban landscape. Pearson's early work understood the theory as an application, an addition to the principles of functionality and aesthetics. Over time, the theory has developed into a defining paradigm, increasingly pervasive in all areas of art and design, particularly those that have to do with space. Stage set design, exhibitions, events, the private home and public space are now included, as well as the mediating space in film and gaming.

Interaktive Tapete

In all seinen Arbeiten entwickelt Christopher Pearson eine Theorie medialer Räume, die durch „Ikonographierung und Zeichengebung" charakterisiert sind. In seinem Studium am Royal College of Art geht er wesentlich weiter und beschreibt die Wirkung verschiedener medialer Einflüsse auf die Gestaltung des urbanen Umfeldes. Was in Pearsons ersten Arbeiten noch als Applikation verstanden wurde, als „add on" mit neuer Funktionalität und Ästhetik, wandelte sich in den letzten Jahren zu einem szenografischen Moment intensivsten Ausmaßes und durchdringt zunehmend auch alle Bereiche der künstlerisch-gestalterischen Auseinandersetzung mit räumlichen Bezug: seien es Bühne, Ausstellung, Event, der private und öffentliche Raum und nicht zuletzt der mediale Raum in Film und Spielen.

Papiers peints interactifs

Dans tous ses travaux, Christopher Pearson expose une théorie sur l'espace et ses médias caractérisée par « l'iconographie et le signalant ». Au cours de ses études au Royal College of Art, il est allé encore plus loin dans sa description des effets des diverses interactions sur l'aménagement de l'environnement urbain. Ce qui dans ses premiers travaux pouvait encore être considéré comme un champ d'application, avec une nouvelle fonctionnalité et une nouvelle esthétique, s'est transformé ces dernières années en un moment scénique d'une intensité extrême et pénètre de plus en plus tous les domaines artistiques et l'aménagement de l'espace, qu'il s'agisse de scènes, d'expositions, de manifestations événementielles, d'espace privé ou public, et bien sûr de cinéma et de théâtre.

Wallpaper patterns as global
imagination in a design-oriented
room.

Tapetenmuster im inszenierten
Raum als globale Imagination.

Motif de papier peint dans un
espace mis globalement en scène.

A network of light, sound and
production media play a significant role in Pearson's work.

Vernetzung, Licht-, Ton- und
Projektionsmedien spielen in den
Arbeiten eine wesentliche Rolle.

Les interactions de médias –
lumière, son, projection – jouent
un rôle primordial.

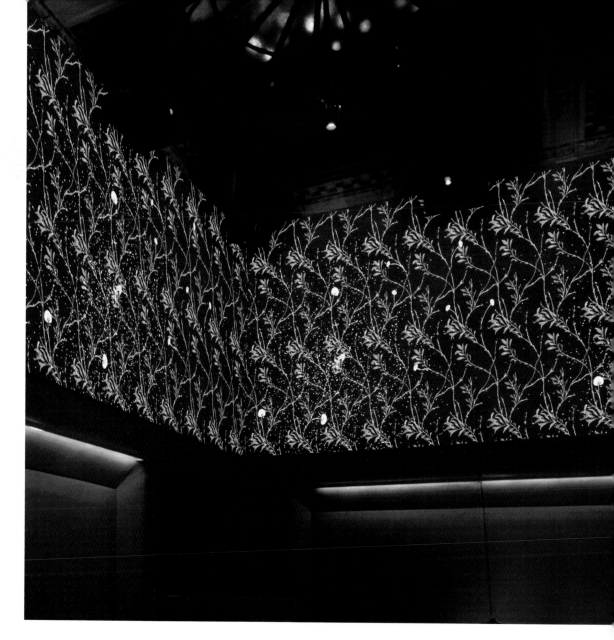

Food, art and music—the restaurant owner, designer and artists joined together in London to create a luxurious temple for the senses. One reason for the success of Sketch is the interactive wallpaper on the walls by Christopher Pearson. The wallpaper was designed to fit the rooms and be adaptable to changes in mood among the guests.

„Food, Art and Music" – Betreiber, Designer und beteiligte Künstler haben in London einen luxuriösen Tempel für alle Sinne geschaffen. Einen Teil des Erfolges von „Sketch" sind die interaktiven Tapetenwände von Christopher Pearson, die eigens für die Räume gestaltet wurden und sich der Stimmung der Gäste anpassen.

« Food, Art and Music » (nourriture, art et musique) : propriétaire, designer et artistes ont réalisé à Londres un temple luxueux qui fait appel à tous les sens. Une partie du succès de Sketch repose sur les papiers peints interactifs de Christopher Pearson, créés uniquement pour ces salles et qui s'adaptent à l'humeur des clients.

Jenny Pilz

Amsel, Drossel, Fink

The wall treatments for the Café Liebling in Berlin were Jenny Pilz's thesis work, early evidence of her sensitive handling of color and form. This project, which she calls Amsel, Drossel, Fink, incorporates the characteristics of the wall itself into the wallpaper design. The screen-painted silk wallpaper is adorned with simple bird motifs that evolve out of elements of floral motifs at the base of the wall, to then rise up and fly free. Expanding ink (puff) is used to print the motifs in relief, projecting out slightly from the wallpaper. Since the motifs are the same color as the background, the difference in planes is what makes them visible at all. Alongside the wallpaper, the motifs leave the wallpaper to be impressed in a concrete wall section, continuing the wallpaper pattern. The upholstery buttons on the banquette benches are yet another reference to birds.

Amsel, Drossel, Fink

Bereits die Diplomarbeit von Jenny Pilz, die Wandgestaltung des Café Liebling in Berlin, zeigt ihren feinfühligen Umgang mit Farben und Formen. Beim Projekt mit dem Namen Amsel, Drossel, Fink wird die Wand mit ihren Eigenschaften bewusst in die Gestaltung der Tapete mit einbezogen. Die im Siebdruck entstandenen Seidentapeten zeigen schlichte Vogelmotive, die im unteren Bereich wie Blüten angeordnet sind, sich nach oben hin immer weiter auflösen bis schließlich die Vögel auf der Tapete frei fliegend verteilt sind. Durch Expansionsfarbe treten die Motive aus der Tapete plastisch hervor und werden so überhaupt erst sichtbar, da diese der Stofffarbe entsprechen. Neben der Tapete verlassen die Motive die Seide und finden sich als Abdrücke im Beton wieder, so dass das Muster in der Wand weiter verläuft. Ein weiteres Zitat der Vögel findet sich in den bestickten Polsterknöpfen.

Amsel, Drossel, Fink

La partie concrète de l'examen de fin d'études de Jenny Pilz – la décoration des murs du Café Liebling à Berlin – dévoile déjà la sensibilité de la créatrice pour les couleurs et les formes. Dans le projet appelé *Amsel, Drossel, Fink* (merle, grive et pinson), les particularités du mur ont été prises en compte pour la réalisation de la tapisserie. Le papier peint en soie créé selon le procédé de sérigraphie montre des motifs élémentaires d'oiseaux. Groupés sous la forme de fleurs en bas de la tapisserie, les oiseaux se séparent peu à peu en remontant le plan vertical pour voler librement dans la partie supérieure de la tapisserie. La couleur des motifs s'accentue au fur et à mesure qu'ils s'élèvent sur la tapisserie jusqu'à ce que les oiseaux prennent une nuance plus foncée sur le fond clair et deviennent visibles en haut du papier peint. Le motif quitte le papier peint en soie pour se retrouver gravé sur le mur en béton, assurant ainsi une continuité au décor. Des oiseaux ornent également les capitons des banquettes.

The glass facade of Bar Babette in Central Berlin serves as a temporary surface for wallpaper. The linear motif on the screen-printed wallpaper is perforated in different parts of the design. Wallpapering gives this otherwise very open room an atmosphere of intimacy. The cut outs in the motifs let it open up again.

In der Bar Babette in Berlin-Mitte wird die Glasfassade temporär zum Trägermaterial der Tapete. Das Motiv der im Siebdruck entstandenen Tapete ist neben den bedruckten Linien gleichzeitig perforiert. Dem sonst sehr offenen Raum wird durch die Tapezierung eine Intimität gegeben, welche sich durch das Herauslösen der einzelnen Elemente wieder öffnet.

Dans le bar Babette situé au cœur de Berlin, une partie de la façade de verre sert également de support à la tapisserie. Le motif du papier peint réalisé selon le procédé de sérigraphie présente des lignes imprimées et des perforations. La tapisserie apporte une intimité à cet espace très ouvert.

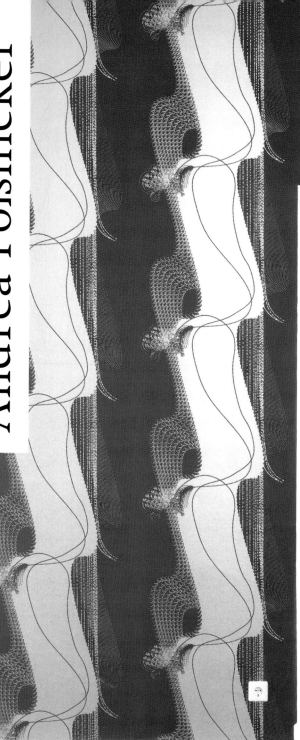

pvanb, Shed*Light

For Andrea Pössnicker, wallpaper is not just paper for the wall, but an interior design concept characteristic of life in a modern castle. Her artistic motifs dominate the entire room and include fashion, textiles, illumination and furniture along with wall treatments. The wallpaper collections are conceived as conceptual works, works that tell stories. The motifs look like mere decoration at first glance, but on second glance, hidden messages come through. The wallpaper encompasses both social themes and personal experiences of the designer. Erotic scenes are typical, with pin-up girls lying under apple trees, cryptic typography, faux romantic landscapes and secret dedications.

pvanb, Shed*Light

Bei Andrea Pößnicker wird Tapete nicht als Papier für die Wand definiert, sondern ist ein Interieurkonzept, welches durch das Leben in einem modernen Schloss charakterisiert werden kann. Die künstlerischen Motive übernehmen den gesamten Raum und in Folge dessen hat sie auch Mode, Textilien, Leuchten und Möbel entwickelt. Die Tapeten-Kollektionen sind Konzept-Arbeiten und erzählen Geschichten. Auf den ersten Blick sehen sie aus wie „Dekorationen", aber der zweite Blick zeigt verborgene Botschaften. In ihren Tapeten bezieht die Designerin gesellschaftliche Themen und persönliche Erfahrungen mit ein. Typisch sind zum Beispiel versteckte erotische Szenen, Pin-ups die unter Apfelbäumen liegen, kryptische Typographien, vermeintlich romantische Landschaften und versteckte Widmungen.

pvanb, Shed*Light

Pour Andrea Pößnicker, la tapisserie n'est pas un simple revêtement mural de papier, mais la conception d'un intérieur qui s'apparenterait à un château moderne. Les motifs artistiques prennent possession de l'espace pour lequel la créatrice a également conçu des textiles, des lampes et du mobilier. Ses collections de papiers peints sont conceptuelles et racontent des histoires. À première vue, la tapisserie ne semble que décorative, mais après une observation minutieuse, on y découvre des messages cachés. La créatrice introduit des sujets de société et des expériences personnelles dans ses papiers peints. Parmi les motifs typiques : les scènes érotiques, les pin-up étendues sous des pommiers, des typographies cryptiques, des paysages faussement romantiques et des dédicaces secrètes.

Wallpapers achieve more than simply covering a wall.

Tapeten mit denen man mehr erreicht als nur eine Wand zu gestalten.

Des papiers peints qui sont plus qu'un simple décor.

The color lies thick upon the wallpaper, with motifs block printed on high quality paper.

Schwer steht die Farbe auf den Tapeten, die auf edlem Papier von Hand gedruckt sind.

Les couleurs se détachent sur le papier peint haut de gamme, imprimé manuellement.

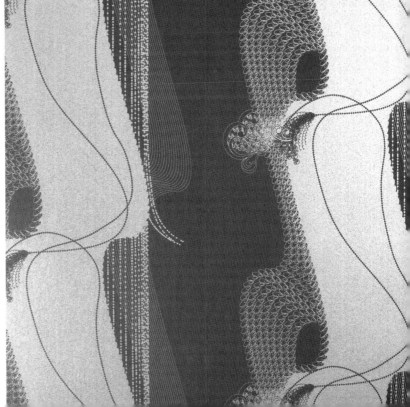

In November 2004 Pössnicker began Shed*Light, an outdoor installation in collaboration with the Museum of Welsh Life in Cardiff, Wales. The project traveled from there to the ARCO Exhibition in Madrid, after which it toured Europe. Shed*Light included wallpaper designed by Pössnicker and the artist Marc Rees, working with architect Benedict Anderson.

Im November 2004 startete mit Shed*Light eine Outdoor-Installation in Zusammenarbeit mit dem Museum of Welsh Life (St Fagans, Cardiff, Wales). Das Projekt ging von dort aus auf die Madrid ARCO Exhibition und tourte danach durch Europa. Shed*Light wurde mit Tapeten von Andrea Pößnicker in Zusammenarbeit mit dem Künstler Marc Rees und dem Architekten Benedict Anderson realisiert.

En novembre 2004, Shed*Light, une installation en plein air, était conçue en collaboration avec le Museum of Welsh Life (St Fagans, Cardiff, Pays de Galles). Le projet fut ensuite présenté à l'exposition ARCO à Madrid avant de partir en tournée à travers l'Europe. Shed*Light a été réalisé avec des papiers peints d'Andrea Pößnicker, et la collaboration de l'artiste Marc Rees et de l'architecte Benedict Anderson.

Hugo Boss AG

Based in Stuttgart with satellites in Zurich and Berlin, Projekttriangle is a studio devoted to communication design. It works on new means of cultural expression and communications forms using analog and digital media in both freeform and applied projects in the fields of culture, science and research. In the process, projecttriangle generates scenarios and produces aesthetic objects while reinterpreting the paradigms of classical design. The goal is to provide a face for things, themes and organizations. Hugo Boss AG hired the studio for the graphic interior design of the new Orange Monostore in Manheim. The result was a 40 foot/12 m high wall installation consisting of 14 individual panels covered in screen-printed fabric, along with 24 broadcasting monitors. The installation formed the center of the 3-storey high, 1,300 sq foot/400 sq m shop. Other surfaces, furniture and walls also received creative treatment.

Hugo Boss AG

Projekttriangle ist ein Designstudio für Informationsgestaltung aus Stuttgart mit Satelliten in Zürich und Berlin. Sie erarbeiten in freien und angewandten Projekten neue kulturelle Ausdrucks- und Kommunikationsformen analoger und digitaler Medien im Bereich Kultur, Wirtschaft und Forschung. Dabei werden szenische Welten und ästhetische Zustände generiert und klassisches Design wird neu interpretiert. Mit dem Ziel, den Dingen, den Themen, den Organisationen ein Gesicht zu geben. Für den neuen Orange Monostore in Mannheim wurden Sie durch die Hugo Boss AG erneut mit der grafischen Raumgestaltung beauftragt. Eine über 12 Meter hohe Wandinstallation, bestehend aus 14 im Siebdruck hergestellte Einzelplatten und 24 bespielten Monitoren, bildet das Zentrum des über 3 Stockwerke hohen und 400 m² großen Shops. Desweiteren wurden Umkleiden, Möbel und Wände gestalterisch bespielt.

Hugo Boss AG

Spécialisée dans le design de l'information, la firme Projekttriangle a son siège à Stuttgart et des dépendances à Zurich et à Berlin. Dans le cadre de leurs projets, le groupe crée de nouvelles formes culturelles de communication des médias analogiques et numériques dans les secteurs de la culture, de l'économie et de la recherche. Des univers sont mis en scène, des ordres esthétiques prennent forme et des motifs classiques reçoivent une nouvelle interprétation. L'objectif est de donner une physionomie aux choses, aux thèmes, aux structures. La société Hugo Boss a confié à Projekttriangle l'aménagement graphique du nouvel Orange Monostore à Mannheim. Une installation murale de plus de 12 m de haut, composée de 14 panneaux individuels élaborés à partir d'un procédé de sérigraphie et de 24 moniteurs reproduisant le décor, constitue le centre du magasin d'une superficie de 400 m² sur trois étages. Les cabines d'essayage, le mobilier et les murs ont une décoration assortie à l'installation.

The new Concept Store in Shanghai is decorated with an over 20 foot/6 m high screen-printed fantasy tree. The typographic woodcut prints help define the "German-ness" of the motifs in the changing rooms. Life-size images of birds were imprinted on the walls using traditional wooden stamps.

Für den neuen Concept Store in Shanghai wurde ein über sechs Meter großer Fantasiebaum illustriert und im Siebdruck realisiert. Typografische Holzschnitzereien zieren die mit goldenen „deutschen" Motiven bedruckten Umkleidekabinen. Zusätzlich wurde ein traditionelles Holzstempelset bestehend aus 10 deutschen Sing- und Waldvögeln in Originalgröße realisiert.

Réalisée en sérigraphie, l'image stylisée d'un arbre de plus de 6 m de haut décore le nouveau *concept store* de Shanghai. Des gravures sur bois typographiques ornent les cabines d'essayage aux murs revêtus de motifs dorés « allemands ». En outre, a été réalisé un set traditionnel de tampons de bois figurant 10 oiseaux chanteurs allemands en grandeur nature.

A fish. Many fish forming a school create a wall pattern.

Ein Fisch. Viele Fische ergeben einen Schwarm als Wandmotiv.

Un banc de poissons forme un motif mural.

Traditionally produced typographic stamps, made by hand.

Handwerklich und traditionell hergestellte Stempel.

Des tampons typographiques fabriqués selon des méthodes traditionnelles artisanales.

Light-colored wood, steel scaffolding wrapped in bands of fabric and a changing booth in the jeans fitting room structure the divergent space. The logo of the flagship store gives the walls a sense of lightness and exhilaration.

Helle Hölzer, mit Stoffbändern ummantelte Stahlgerüste und eine Fashionbox in Jeansauskleidung gliedern den divergenten Raum. Die bereits eingesetzten, grafischen Wandmotive der Flagshipstores vermitteln den Wänden etwas Leichtes und Beschwingtes.

Des bois clairs, une charpente en acier enveloppée de bandes d'étoffe et une *fashionbox* revêtue de jean articulent l'espace divergent. Les dessins muraux faisant déjà partie de la décoration des *flagship stores* confèrent aux parois une impression de légèreté et de gaieté.

RaiserLopesDesigners

EspressoBar

EspressoBar radiates lightness and peace in the midst of the activity and industriousness of the outlet stores in Metzingen, inviting the shopper to come in and spend some time. The contrasts between inside and outside, the colors, structure and stucco structure behind the metallic surfaces are perfectly realized, from the concrete floor to the arrangement of the colored stripes. The styles and current trends of the fashion industry are referred to in a coherent, colorful way. This is the right place to rest body and soul in an agreeable atmosphere.

EspressoBar

Bei der Fülle von Aktivitäten und der Betriebsamkeit, die in den Shop-Outlets in Metzingen vorherrschen, strahlt die EspressoBar Leichtigkeit und Ruhe aus und lädt zum Verweilen ein. Die Wechselwirkung von Innen und Außen, von Farbe, Struktur und Oberfläche, inszeniert durch strukturierten Putz in Kontrast zu metallischen Oberflächen und zum Betonboden sowie die Kombination mit Farbstreifen, die an Mode und an Farbtrends der Mode-Industrie erinnern, ist in stimmiger und farbenfröhlicher Weise perfekt gelungen. Der richtige Platz um sich in angenehmer Atmosphäre Seele und Beine baumeln zu lassen.

EspressoBar

Au cœur de l'animation qui règne dans le centre commercial « Shop-Outlets » à Metzingen, l'Espresso-Bar est un îlot de paix et de clarté qui invite à la détente. Cet ensemble très réussi, tant au niveau des matériaux que des couleurs, est le fruit de multiples interactions : espace intérieur, espace extérieur, couleurs, surfaces. Les murs sont mis en scène à l'aide d'un crépi structuré, qui contraste avec le métal des tables et des comptoirs et le béton du sol, ainsi qu'avec des raies de couleur qui suivent les tendances de l'industrie de la mode. L'EspressoBar offre une ambiance idéale pour la détente de l'esprit et du corps.

The days in which it was enough simply to whitewash the walls are long past. In addition to aspects like ambience and lighting, temperature and air quality also have an effect on a room. In high-end hotels and gastronomy, these qualities are in great demand.

Die Zeiten, in denen es genügte, die Wände einfach weiß zu tünchen sind längst vorbei. Neben Aspekten wie Ambiente und Belichtung haben auch Temperatur und Luftqualität einen wesentlichen Einfluss auf die Räume. Gerade im Premiumsegment wie in Hotels und Gastronomie sind diese Eigenschaften gefragt.

L'époque où il suffisait de peindre les murs en blanc est depuis longtemps révolue. Des aspects tels que l'ambiance et l'éclairage, la température et la qualité de l'air ont pris de plus en plus d'importance dans l'aménagement des espaces intérieurs et sont surtout exigés dans les secteurs haut de gamme comme l'hôtellerie et la gastronomie.

Rasch

Bauhaus

The Bauhaus wallpaper collection is the one industrial product that reflects the 1928 collaboration with the Dessau Bauhaus group in a new, updated form. Bauhaus wallpaper continued to sell after 1933, outliving the term "Bauhaus" after the Nazi government shut down the atelier and design school. During the postwar period, the designs were continually re-launched according to the requirements of the times. Bauhaus wallpaper communicates an elegant simplicity, superior quality and persuasive modernity that are still in demand today. The great traditions and timeless style of the design house live on in the structure, surfaces and colors, all well in tune with the demands of contemporary interior decor.

Bauhaus

Die Bauhaus-Tapetenkollektion ist das einzige industrielle Produkt, das seit der Zusammenarbeit mit dem Bauhaus in Dessau, im Jahre 1928, immer wieder in aktualisierter Form das Bauhaus-Gedankengut widerspiegelt. Auch nach 1933 behauptete sich die Bauhaus-Tapete und mit ihr überlebte sogar der Begriff Bauhaus, nachdem die Schule unter dem Druck der nationalsozialistischen Machthaber schließen musste. Seit den Nachkriegsjahren immer wieder neu aufgelegt und den Bedürfnissen der Zeit angepasst, vermittelt die Bauhaus-Tapete bis heute jene elegante Einfachheit, anspruchsvolle Qualität und überzeugende Modernität, die die Produkte des Bauhauses auszeichnen. Die große Tradition des Hauses lebt in der zeitlos-dezenten Haltung von Struktur, Oberfläche und Farbe weiter und verbindet sich mit heutigen Ansprüchen an ein zeitgemäßes Interieur.

Bauhaus

La collection de papiers peints Bauhaus est l'unique produit industriel qui, depuis la collaboration de l'industrie avec le mouvement du Bauhaus à Dessau, en 1928, ne cesse de remémorer les idées du Bauhaus sous des formes actualisées. Alors qu'en 1933, la célèbre école devait fermer ses portes sous la pression du pouvoir national-socialiste, la tapisserie Bauhaus a continué d'exister et avec elle l'esprit du Bauhaus. Depuis l'après-guerre, la production ne s'est jamais interrompue en s'adaptant aux besoins des générations nouvelles. Les papiers peints Bauhaus sont aujourd'hui encore synonymes d'élégante simplicité, de grande qualité et de modernité à l'image des autres ouvrages du Bauhaus. L'héritage transmis par cette école se manifeste dans le traitement intemporel et sobre des structures, surfaces et couleurs, en accord avec les exigences requises dans les intérieurs contemporains.

Rarely has a Bauhaus collection come so close to the original intent of the Bauhaus philosophy, while remaining very modern. The new Bauhaus-Collection includes, among others, wallpapers based on original designs by Walter Gropius, the founder and first director of the Weimer Bauhaus group.

Selten zuvor war eine Bauhaus-Tapetenkollektion so nah an den Ursprüngen des Bauhaus-Gedankens orientiert und zugleich so modern. Die neue Bauhaus-Kollektion beinhaltet unter anderem Tapeten, die auf Original-Entwürfen von Walter Gropius, dem ersten Direktor des Bauhauses in Weimar basieren.

Peu de collections précédentes de papiers peints Bauhaus ont été aussi proches de cet esprit, tout en restant très moderne. La nouvelle collection Bauhaus comprend entre autres des dessins originaux de Walter Gropius, le premier directeur de l'école, alors située à Weimar.

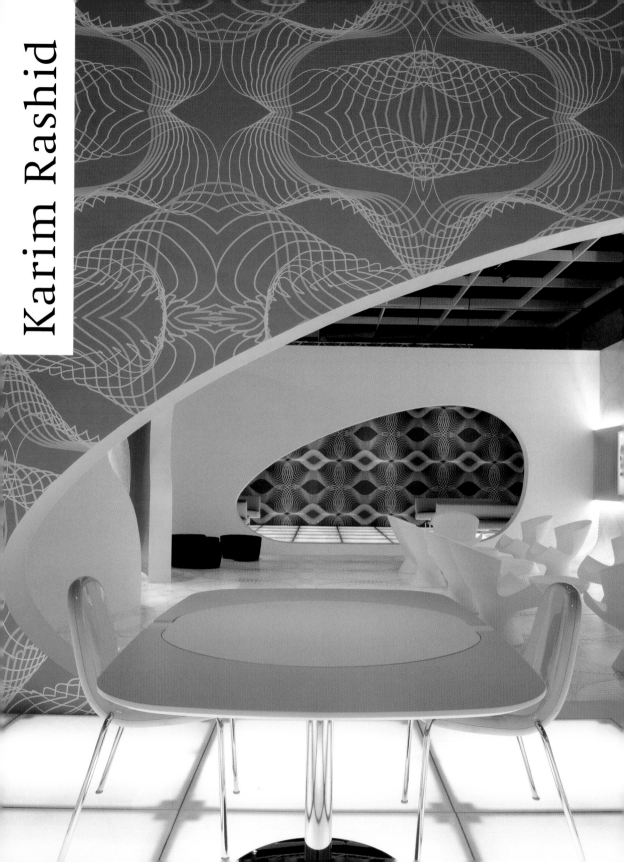

Karim Rashid

Deutsche Bank Lounge

In celebration of the 40th jubilee of ArtCologne, Deutsche Bank exhibited its art in an extraordinary presentation space. Karim Rashid designed the gallery and lounge. The designer, best known for his trendy, flashy products and interiors, created a distinctive space. The curved walls were covered in wallpaper with computer-generated, three dimensional patterns. Large, amorphous-shaped portals, painted fluorescent yellow, draw the eye to the bar on the right and meeting area to the left. Psychedelic patterns in pink and blue adorn walls bathed in light from the illuminated floor.

Deutsche Bank Lounge

Zum 40jährigen Jubiläum der ArtCologne präsentierte sich die Deutsche Bank Kunstsammlung mit einem außergewöhnlichen Stand. Die Galerie und Lounge wurde von Karim Rashid entworfen. Der Designer, bekannt durch seine meist poppigen und grellen Produkte und Interiors, schuf einen unverwechselbaren Raum. Die geschwungenen Wände wurden mit Tapeten bestückt, die computergenerierte, dreidimensionale Muster aufwiesen. Große amorphe Öffnungen, in fluoreszierendem gelb gestrichen, ließen Blickbeziehungen zu den rechts und links befindlichen Bar- bzw. Meetingbereichen zu. Psychedelische Muster in pink und blau schmückten hier die Wände und wurden durch die beleuchteten Böden ins rechte Licht gerückt.

Deutsche Bank Lounge

À l'occasion du 40ᵉ anniversaire de la foire ArtCologne, le stand qui abritait la collection d'art de la Deutsche Bank a été très remarqué. Célèbre pour ses ouvrages et aménagements intérieurs très colorés, pour la plupart de facture pop, le designer Karim Raschid a signé la galerie et le salon. Unique en son genre, son style se révèle dans les murs revêtus de papiers peints aux motifs tridimensionnels créés par ordinateur. De vastes ouvertures aux lignes fluides, peintes en jaune fluorescent, donnent sur le bar et autres zones d'échanges. Dans cet espace, des motifs psychédéliques dans les tons rose et bleu décorent les murs et sont mis en valeur par des éclairages au sol.

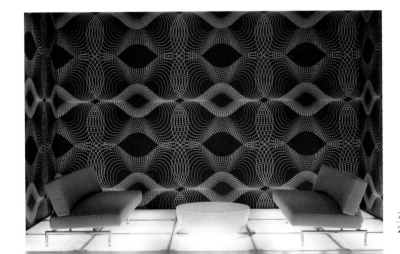

Olivier Jean Sebastian

Insectofobia

The first impression is not the only one that counts! The pattern collection Insectofobia goes deeper thus deserving a second look. Upon closer observation, the ornamental and graphic elements transform into swarms of insects moving in unison across the surface of the wallpaper. The metamorphosis is perfect. Exotic flowers suddenly reveal their true nature as colorful dragonflies, beetles, spiders and ants, all dancing rhythmically across the wall. Olivier Jean Sebastian creates a range of innovative, imaginative patterns full of hidden, surprising details that have a unique story to tell. The distinctive color scheme and formal language of Insectofobia crawls, rustles, buzzes—and meets with approval.

Insectofobia

Nicht nur der erste Eindruck zählt! Auch der zweite lässt tief blicken, denn die Musterkollektion Insectofobia hat es in sich. Die ornamentalen und grafischen Formen verwandeln sich bei näherer Betrachtung in Scharen von Insekten, die sich im Rapport über die Oberfläche bewegen. Die Metamorphose ist perfekt: exotische Blumen entpuppen sich plötzlich als bunte Libellen. Käfer, Spinnen und Ameisen formieren sich zu leuchtenden Kreisen und Rauten. Die Gliederfüßer erobern den Raum und tanzen rhythmisch über die Fläche. Olivier Jean Sebastian präsentiert eine Reihe von innovativen, phantasievollen Mustern, die voller überraschender Details stecken und ihre ganz eigene Geschichte erzählen. Insectofobia krabbelt, raschelt, summt und besticht durch ihre ungewöhnliche Farb- und Formsprache.

Insectofobia

Ici, ce n'est pas uniquement la première impression qui compte ! Une observation plus attentive permet d'entrevoir des profondeurs insoupçonnées. La collection de papier peint *Insectofobia* est vraiment insolite. Les formes graphiques et ornementales se muent en nuées d'insectes qui semblent exécuter des figures de ballet sur la tapisserie. La métamorphose est parfaite : des fleurs exotiques se transforment soudain en libellules colorées. Scarabées, araignées et fourmis se rassemblent pour former des cercles et des losanges. Tous ces arthropodes se sont emparés de l'espace où ils évoluent rythmiquement. Olivier Jean Sebastian présente toute une série de motifs inédits, pleins de fantaisie et de détails surprenants. Chaque tapisserie raconte une histoire. Cette collection pique la curiosité par son interprétation des formes et des couleurs.

Ich denke sowieso mit dem Knie

Joseph Beuys

Wall tattoos

Silbensalon invented the wall tattoo. Designed to showcase distinctive quotes, wall tattoos decorate living spaces while ensuring that the right word covers the right spot. Whether used in a domestic context or in businesses, hotels, shops or restaurants, the quotes take the viewer by surprise while giving a room identity. The designers Jutta Reichert and Martina Gallant offer both illustrated words and graphic designs. The texts are printed on very thin, self-sticking plastic sheets that, once applied, look like they were painted on. They let the walls do the talking. The texts come complete, fully formatted and laid out in one piece, making them easy stick to the wall—and just as easy to remove. The broad range of color palettes and texts are appropriate for any living area.

Wandtattoo

Der Silbensalon, Erfinder der Wandtattoos, gestaltet mit Hilfe von ungewöhnlichen Zitaten Lebensräume neu und dekoriert das fehlende Wort an den richtigen Fleck. Ob im privaten Bereich oder in Firmen, Hotels, Shops oder Restaurant, die Sprüche überraschen und geben den Räumen eine eigene Identität. Die Designerinnen Jutta Reichert und Martina Gallant bieten Wortkunst und Grafikobjekte. Die Schriften sind hauchdünne, selbstklebende Spezialfolien, die wie gemalt, Wände sprechen lassen. Die Texte werden zum einfachen Ankleben vorpositioniert auf einer Trägerfolie geliefert (und lassen sich ebenso leicht wieder entfernen). Eine breite Farb- und Schriftenpalette passt sich allen Wohnbereichen an.

Tatouage mural

Silbensalon, créateur du tatouage mural, transforme les espaces intérieurs au moyen de citations insolites et décore quand le verbe fait défaut. Habitations, entreprises, hôtels, magasins ou restaurants, les citations surprennent et confèrent aux espaces leur propre identité. Les créatrices Jutta Reichert et Martina Gallant œuvrent par les mots et les objets graphiques. Élaborées dans un film approprié très fin et autocollant, les lettres, à l'image de la calligraphie, donnent la parole aux murs. Les textes sont livrés sur support plastifié. Déjà positionnés, ils sont faciles à coller (et à décoller au besoin). Une large palette de coloris et de lettres permet une décoration adaptée à chaque intérieur.

No Sports

Winston Churchill

A favorite motto or beloved verse, rude proverb or intellectual quote.

Lebensmotto oder Lieblings-gedicht, frecher Spruch oder intelligentes Zitat.

Devises ou poèmes favoris, bons mots ou citations philosophiques.

Graphic designs, illustrations and nursery rhymes—the possibilities are endless.

Grafik, Illustration, Kinder-reime – die Möglichkeiten sind unbegrenzt ...

Dessins, illustrations, comptines : les possibilités sont illimitées...

Dem Heiteren erscheint die Welt auch heiter.

In ein Haus,

in dem die Freude lebt,

zieht auch das Glück gern ein.

japanisch

Ich kann,
weil ich will,
was ich muss.

Immanuel Kant

Soonsalon

Miss White

The wallpapers designed by the Dutch firm Soonsalon are at first glance not particularly unusual. Patterns utilizing bold colors and shapes dominate the collection. But should the viewer move in closer, the true character of the decor reveals itself: posed, beckoning men and women, repeated over and over again to form a striking pattern. The designer began the 2006 renovation of the Hotel and Restaurant Zandhorst by choosing this wallpaper. The 51 rooms are all decorated differently, each uniquely furnished. Two rooms have the design Miss White on the walls. A million chorus girls dance against a black background, making a stay in those rooms into a sensual experience.

Miss White

Die Tapeten der Designerin des niederländischen Unternehmens Soonsalon wirken auf den ersten Blick nicht ungewöhnlich: Muster in starken Farben und Formen dominieren die Tapeten-Kollektion. Geht der Betrachter jedoch näher heran, offenbart sich ihm der wahre Charakter der Dekore: Posierende und herausfordernde Damen und Herren ergeben, vielfach wiederholt, das aparte Muster. Mit einer Auswahl dieser Tapeten begannen die Designer Anfang 2006 mit der Renovierung des Hotels und Restaurants Zandhorst. Die 51 Zimmer wurden alle unterschiedlich eingerichtet, so dass jedes zum Unikat wurde. In zwei Räumen verwendeten die Gestalter die Miss White Tapete. Auf schwarzem Grund tanzen hier Millionen Revuetänzerinnen und lassen den Aufenthalt in den Zimmer zu einem sinnlichen Erlebnis werden.

Miss White

Les papiers peints du designer de l'entreprise néerlandaise Soonsalon ne semblent pas exceptionnels au premier regard : des dessins aux coloris puissants dominent la collection. Mais en s'approchant de la tapisserie, l'observateur attentif découvre le véritable caractère des motifs. Les décors ont du cachet : ils sont constitués de rangées de figures masculines et féminines dans des poses provocantes. Les designers ont choisi des papiers peints de cette série pour les travaux de rénovation de l'hôtel et du restaurant Zandhorst effectués en 2006. Chacune des 51 chambres a un décor et un aménagement individuels. Les architectes d'intérieur ont utilisé la tapisserie *Miss White* dans deux chambres. Le motif est suggestif : des millions de danseuses de variétés pirouettent sur un fond noir. Des murs se dégage une sensualité qui se répand dans tout l'espace.

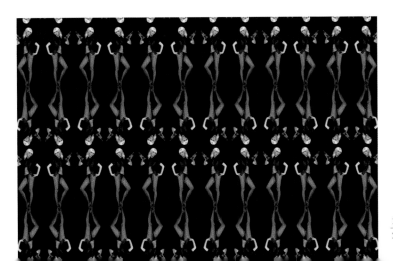

Schwarzer Laubfrosch, Orangerie

The architects from Splitterwerk always work with large-scale patterns. It is the scale that makes them so surprising and special. The best-known example is the apartment building called Schwarzer Laubfrosch (black tree frog). The vine leaf motif covers not only the outside of the building, but also the floor, walls and ceilings of the corridor. The apartments themselves are unusual. Each wall has an oversized sliding door, behind which the bathroom, kitchenette, bed and table lie concealed. When the doors are closed, the inhabitant has a long, empty room at his or her own disposal. As needed, one or more doors can be opened and the furnishings unfolded or stored out of the way.

Schwarzer Laubfrosch, Orangerie

Die Architekten von Splitterwerk arbeiten immer wieder mit großflächig angebrachten Mustern. Das Überraschende und Besondere sind allerdings die Ausmaße. Bekanntestes Beispiel ist der schwarze Laubfrosch. Nicht nur die gesamte Außenhaut des Gebäudes, sondern auch die Wände, Böden und Decken der Korridore sind mit dem Hauptmotiv, Weinranken, bedruckt. Die Wohnungen sind außergewöhnlich: an jeder Wand befinden sich riesige Schiebetüren hinter denen sich Bad, Küchenzeile, Bett und Tisch verbergen. Sind die Türen geschlossen, hat der Bewohner einen länglichen, leeren Raum zur freien Verfügung. Je nach Bedarf können diese geöffnet und die Möbel herausgeklappt oder geschoben werden.

Schwarzer Laubfrosch, Orangerie

Les architectes de Splitterwerk ont l'habitude de travailler avec des motifs sur de vastes surfaces. La superficie recouverte peut surprendre par son ampleur, ainsi qu'en témoigne le bâtiment appelé « Schwarzer Laubfrosch » (le rainette noire) l'exemple le plus connu. Le motif principal présentant des feuilles de vigne grimpante habille non seulement les murs extérieurs de l'immeuble, mais aussi les murs, les plafonds et les sols des corridors. Les appartements sortent de l'ordinaire : chaque mur est doté d'immenses portes coulissantes qui cachent le bain, les éléments de cuisine, le lit et la table. Quand elles sont fermées, le résident dispose d'une longue pièce vide qu'il peut arranger à son goût. Selon les besoins, on peut ouvrir les portes, et déplier ou bouger les meubles.

The Blue Shell is a one-room apartment in Schwarzer Laubfrosch building.

Die Blaue Muschel ist ein Ein-Zimmer-Apartment im Schwarzen Laubfrosch.

Le Coquillage bleu est le nom d'un des studios du Schwarzer Laubfrosch.

Schwarzer Laubfrosch feels more like a computer animation than an apartment building.

Man wähnt sich eher in einer Computeranimation als in einem Wohnhaus.

On se croirait plutôt dans un jeu vidéo que dans un appartement.

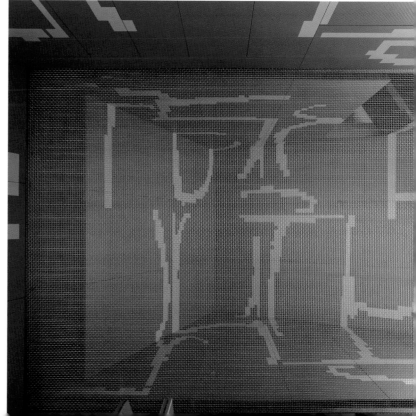

The Orangerie was designed as an event hall for banquets, festive meals and chamber music concerts. The walls, floor and ceilings in the main room are papered with a variety of reflective gold tones. The goal was to create an opulent, ornamental wall treatment using mirror effects so as to make the boundaries of the room disappear.

Die Orangerie wird als repräsentativer Veranstaltungssaal für Bankette, Festtafeln und Kammerkonzerte genutzt. Die Wand-, Boden- und Deckenbeschichtung im Veranstaltungssaal erfolgte mit unterschiedlich reflektierenden Goldtönen. Das Ziel war mit einer opulenten, ornamentalen Wandgestaltung und durch den Einsatz von Spiegeleffekten, die den Raum begrenzenden Raumkanten verschwinden zu lassen.

L'Orangerie est une salle pour banquets, réceptions et concerts de musique de chambre. Les murs, le sol et le plafond sont recouverts de diverses nuances d'or. On a voulu faire disparaître les angles de la salle par le biais d'un revêtement mural opulent et d'effets miroitants.

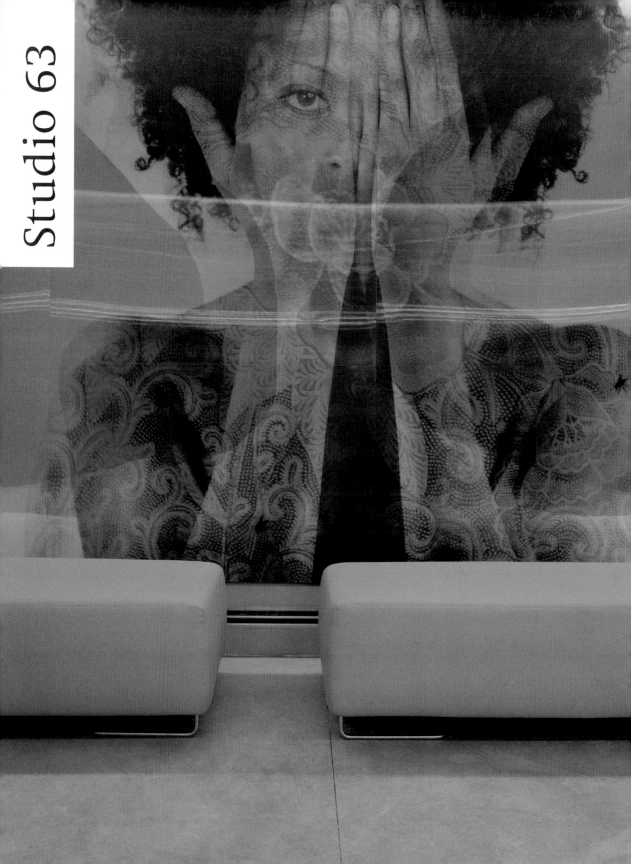

Studio 63

Miss Sixty Hotel

With neon colors, bold seventies design, handmade wallpaper patterns, and graffiti with no end of cool statements like "someone died in this room," the Miss Sixty hotel in the chic spa town of Riccione, Italy attracts a young crowd of fashionistas, club celebrities, models and photographers from all over the world. Miss Sixty cofounder Wichy Hassan worked with over sixty young artists and the Studio63 design firm to create a hip, four-star hotel. The artistic concept carries through into all design areas: to translate the brand's unique style into architecture and interior decoration.

Miss Sixty Hotel

Mit grellen Farben, auffälligem Seventies-Design, handgearbeiteten Tapetenmustern, Graffiti und jeder Menge cooler Wandsprüche wie „Someone died in this room" lockt das erste Miss-Sixty-Hotel junge Modebegeisterte, Szenengänger, Models und Fotografen aus aller Welt in Italiens derzeit angesagtesten Badeort Riccione. Zusammen mit 30 jungen Künstlern hat Miss-Sixty-Mitbegründer Wichy Hassan und die Designer von Studio63 hier ein poppiges Vier-Sterne- Hotel entworfen. Das künstlerische Konzept des Hotels verfolgt dabei eine klare Linie: Es ist die Übersetzung der firmeneigenen Modephilosophie von Miss Sixty in Architektur und Innenausstattung.

Hôtel Miss Sixty

Le premier hôtel Miss Sixty est situé à Riccione, station balnéaire italienne très en vogue actuellement. Il attire une clientèle internationale, jeune et branchée, composée de mannequins, photographes et autres personnalités du fait de son décor : des couleurs vives, un design années 1970, des motifs muraux réalisés à la main, des graffitis et des citations branchées comme : « someone died in this room » (quelqu'un est mort dans cette chambre). Wichy Hassan, co-fondateur de Miss Sixty, 30 jeunes artistes et les designers de Studio63 ont créé ici un hôtel quatre-étoiles tendance. Les objectifs suivis par la conception artistique étaient très clairs : traduire dans l'architecture et l'aménagement intérieur la philosophie de la marque Miss Sixty.

Words that say it all: introduction, body and climax.

Sätze die alles sagen: Einführung, Hauptteil und Höhepunkt.

Sur les murs, des phrases qui sont tout un programme.

The ambience of the room is enhanced by the sensual presence of wallpaper in contrast with playful details.

Dem sachlichen Zimmerambiente stehen die sinnliche Präsenz der Tapete und die verspielten Details gegenüber.

Les papiers peints chaleureux et les détails décoratifs contrastent avec l'agencement fonctionnel des chambres.

Thermopal

Atlantic Hotel

An extraordinary design concept was made reality at Bremen's Atlantic Hotel "on the race track." In recognition of the race track next door, motifs relating to horseracing are worked into decorative elements throughout the hotel, defining its special character. Thus, the guest is welcomed at a grass-green reception counter in front of a freestanding photographic wallpaper mural showing a racing scene. The directory system uses displays in the form of a jockey's colors to guide the guest through the building. The design experts of Thermopal continue this expressive design concept throughout the hotel. Using digital prints, every imaginable racing-related motif could be printed on any material, regardless of condition.

Atlantic Hotel

Im „Atlantic Hotel an der Galopprennbahn" wurde ein außergewöhnliches Designkonzept verwirklicht: In Anlehnung an die benachbarte Galopprennbahn ziehen Motive des Pferderennsports in Form von dekorativen Elementen die Blicke auf sich und machen den besonderen Charakter des Hauses aus. So wird der Gast von einem grasgrünen Tresen empfangen, kombiniert mit einer frei stehenden Foto-Tapetenwand, die eine Galopprennszene darstellt. Ein Leitsystem aus Aufstellern, grafisch umgesetzt in Form von Jockeytrikots, führt den Gast auf sein Zimmer. Umgesetzt wurde diese ausdrucksstarke Designkonzeption des Hotels mit der Individual-Technik von Thermopal: Dabei wird mittels Digitaldruck jedes denkbare Motiv unabhängig von der Auflage in Schichtstoff verpresst.

Hôtel Atlantic

Une conception design assez insolite a été réalisée à l'hôtel Atlantic. En référence au champ de courses hippiques voisin, des motifs de courses ont été utilisés comme éléments décoratifs. Ils retiennent l'attention et donnent à l'hôtel un caractère particulier. Le client est ainsi accueilli devant un comptoir dont la couleur verte évoque une pelouse et qui est associé à des panneaux panoramiques représentant des scènes de courses. Une installation constituée de représentations graphiques de casaques de jockeys guide les clients vers les chambres. Thermopal a utilisé une technique particulière pour mener à bien ce design très expressif. Quel que soit le support, tous les motifs sont tirés par moyen numérique sur du stratifié.

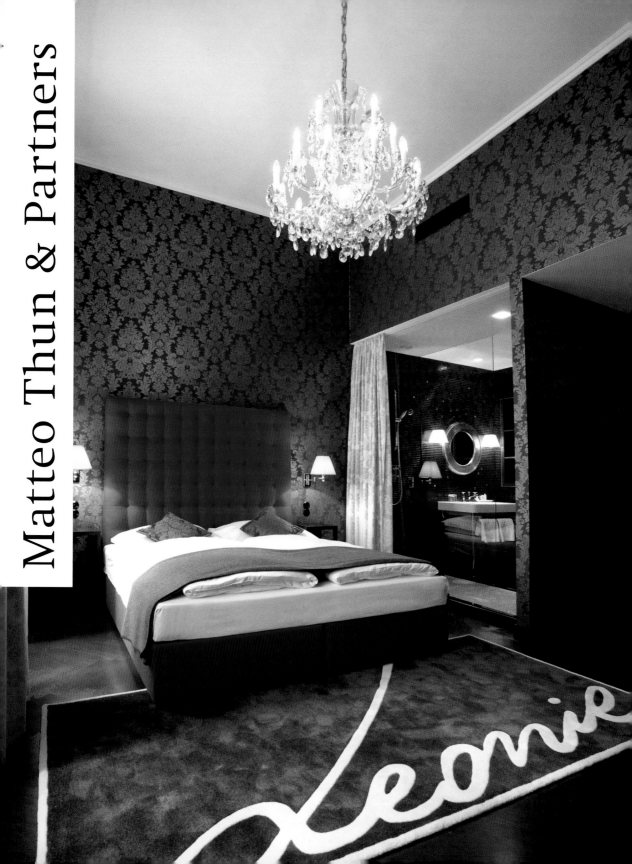

Hotel Altstadt

The Hotel Altstadt is located in a late nineteenth century building in Vienna's seventh district, not far from Spittelberg. Matteo Thun decorated eight of its rooms and a suite. His vision was a new interpretation of the transitional age, the Belle Époque, between the nineteenth and twentieth centuries. The rooms are dominated by dark colors, with panels of stained oak and dark, damask wallpaper as decorative elements. The suite is known as the Master's Chamber. In contrast to the other rooms, its wallpaper is striped and its sofas and armchairs are upholstered in brown leather. The bedcovering remains dark, and the carpet is a deep cognac color. A striking feature of the Master's Chamber is the open bathroom, with a freestanding bathtub on a podium next to the basin and mirror.

Hotel Altstadt

In einem Gebäude aus der Gründerzeit, im 7. Wiener Bezirk, nahe dem Spittelberg, liegt das Hotel Altstadt, dessen acht neue Zimmer und eine Suite von Matteo Thun gestaltet wurden. Seine Vision für die Gestaltung war eine Neuinterpretation zur Zeit der Wende zwischen dem 19. zum 20. Jahrhundert. Die Zimmer sind alle sehr dunkel gehalten, mit Parkett aus gebeizter Eiche und Tapeten aus dunklem Damastmuster als dekoratives Element. Die Suite im Ensemble ist das so genannte Herrenzimmer. Im Unterschied zu den anderen Zimmern ist die Tapete hier gestreift, Sofa und Sessel sind in braunem Leder gepolstert, das Bett ist dunkel gehalten und der Teppich cognacfarben. Auffallend im Herrenzimmer ist das offene Badezimmer, mit einer auf einem Podest frei stehenden Badewanne, neben Waschbecken und Spiegel.

Hôtel Altstadt

L'hôtel Alstadt occupe un édifice de l'époque du Gründerzeit, vers 1870, près du Spittelberg dans le 7e arrondissement de Vienne. Matteo Thun a agencé les huit nouvelles chambres et une suite de l'hôtel en donnant à la période de la fin du XIXe siècle et du début du XXe siècle une interprétation nouvelle. Les parquets en chêne teinté et la tapisserie aux motifs foncés de damas donnent aux chambres l'obscurité recherchée. La suite, nommée « Herrenzimmer » présente une décoration différente des autres chambres. Ici, la tapisserie est à rayures, le canapé et les fauteuils sont recouverts de cuir brun, le lit est également foncé et la moquette couleur cognac. La salle de bains ouverte sur la chambre est intéressante avec une baignoire dressée sur une estrade, un lavabo et un miroir de style Belle Époque.

Kinderparadies

Mateja Vehovar and Stefan Jauslin belong to the generation of younger Swiss architects. In addition to architecture, they also work in landscape design, exhibition design, public space design and artistic installations. The vision of the architects in the design of the children's play space Kinderparadies (Children's Paradise) was to make children's hearts beat faster in a world of shapes and forms far removed from the unimaginative, sober world of shopping centers and other such places. The entire play space is inhabited by every variety of sea creatures. Fish, seahorses, shells and hermit crabs await discovery in every corner: a colorful merry little crowd, happy to share their home with the children.

Kinderparadies

Mateja Vehovar und Stefan Jauslin gehören zur Generation junger Schweizer Architekten. Neben Architekturaufgaben beschäftigen sie sich auch mit Bereichen wie Landschaftsarchitektur, Ausstellungsdesign, Gestaltung des öffentlichen Raumes und künstlerischen Installationen. Das Hauptziel, das die Architekten bei der Gestaltung des Kinderparadieses verfolgten, war Kinderherzen höher schlagen zu lassen und sich durch eine eigene Themen- und Formenwelt von den fantasielosen nüchternen Einrichtungen abzusetzen, wie sie in Einkaufszentren oft anzutreffen sind. Das Ganze wird natürlich von allerlei Meeresgetier bewohnt. Überall gibt es Fische, Seepferdchen, Muscheln oder Taschenkrebse zu entdecken; ein lustiges, buntes Völkchen, das sein Zuhause gerne mit den Kindern teilt.

Paradis pour enfants

Mateja Vehovar et Stefan Jauslin appartiennent à la jeune génération d'architectes suisses. Parallèlement à l'architecture, ils travaillent également dans des domaines tels que l'architecture paysagiste, la conception d'expositions et d'espaces collectifs et les installations artistiques. L'objectif principal qui a accompagné la création de ce paradis pour enfants était d'abord que les enfants l'adorent, et ensuite que les thèmes et les formes le démarquent des aires de jeu sans fantaisie et un peu fades rencontrées trop souvent dans les centres commerciaux. Des animaux marins de toutes sortes constituent les motifs de la décoration. Partout, on peut admirer poissons, hippocampes, coquillages, crabes et pieuvres : un royaume marin ludique et coloré qui ouvre ses portes aux enfants.

All kinds of sea creatures inhabit
the underwater paradise.

Allerlei Meeresgetier bevölkert
das Unterwasserparadies.

Des animaux marins, petits
et grands, peuplent ce paradis
sous-marin.

Diving into adventure in kinderparadies.

Eintauchen ins Abenteuer
Kinderparadies.

Les enfants plongent dans un
monde plein d'aventures.

Digital printing techniques bring increased flexibility and a wealth of new possibilities to freeform design. Wallpaper murals big enough to cover an entire wall are experiencing a renaissance. In this company cafeteria, the photographic wallpaper mural isn't "off the rack." Instead, every wallpaper mural is a one of a kind piece made to measure for individual clients.

Der Digitaldruck mit seiner Flexibilität und Möglichkeit der Einzelfertigung ermöglicht Gestaltern neue Freiheiten. So erleben auf diese Weise wandumspannende Tapetenbilder eine Renaissance. Wie hier in einem Betriebsrestaurant kommt die Fototapete nicht mehr „von der Stange", sie ist ein für den Kunden maßgeschneidertes Unikat.

Grâce à sa flexibilité et son individualité, l'impression numérique donne aux designers de nouvelles libertés dans le domaine de la création. Le panneau panoramique connaît ainsi une renaissance. Il n'est plus acheté tout fait en magasin, mais réalisé sur mesure pour le client, comme ces « fresques » ornant un restaurant d'entreprise.

Design Object Wallpapers

First seen in advertising, textile printing—printing on textile wallpaper—is now one of the most promising digital printing techniques. The perfect print can be achieved to meet any requirements using a wide variety of materials and print fields up to 10 feet/3 m in width. The choice of backing material ranges from lightweight silk blends, to satin or even heavyweight display materials. Almost anything is possible. In addition, the materials themselves can be treated so as to comply with fireproofing regulations. Design models include everything from the Old Masters to modern photography. Graffiti and digital art can be printed large-scale. The most off the wall ideas can be easily produced using the most up to date techniques—causing a sensation!

Tapetenobjekte

In der Werbebranche wurde sie zuerst gesichtet. Nun gehört Textildruck bzw. der Druck auf Textiltapeten zu einem der zukunftsträchtigsten Digitaldruck-Bereiche. Durch eine breite Materialauswahl kann für jede gewünschte Anmutung der perfekte Druck bis zu drei Meter Druckbreite geliefert werden. Die Auswahl der Trägermaterialien reicht vom leichten Fahnenstoff, über Satin oder schweren Displaystoffen. Fast alles ist alles möglich – daneben erfüllen alle Materialien auch die hohen Brandschutzvoraussetzungen. Moderne Fotografie und Gemälde alter Meister dienen als Vorbild, Graffiti und digitale Kunst werden großformatig gedruckt. Schrägste Ideen werden in neuester Technik erstellt und werden für Aufsehen sorgen.

Panneaux décoratifs

Elle a fait sa première apparition pour les besoins de la publicité. Depuis, l'impression sur tapisserie textile connaît un bel essor dans le secteur de l'impression numérique. Grâce à un vaste choix de matériaux, il est possible de réaliser des impressions parfaites, mesurant jusqu'à trois mètres de largeur et pour tous les goûts. Les supports varient du voile léger, pour bannière, au satin et aux lourds tissus d'ameublement. Presque tout est possible. De plus, les matériaux remplissent les normes en vigueur en matière de prévention du feu. Photographies modernes et tableaux de maîtres anciens servent de modèles ; des graffitis et de l'art graphique numérique sont imprimés en grand format. Les idées les plus extravagantes peuvent être réalisées avec ces nouvelles techniques. Le succès de la décoration est assuré.

Wild patterns are waking sleep-
ing beauty walls up from their
long slumber.

Wilde Muster reißen Wände aus
ihrem Dornröschenschlaf.

Des motifs incroyables décorent
ces murs et les arrachent à leur
passivité.

Walls can now be thematically
designed.

So können Wände themenüber-
greifend inszeniert werden.

Le thème est identique mais la
mise en scène est différente.

Marcel Wanders

Lute Suites

The Netherlands is a well-known source of exciting design products, and Marcel Wanders is one of its most famous designers. His furniture designs have always attracted attention, but his vision has always stretched further than the production of individual objects. The Lute Suites represent his interest in comprehensive conceptual interior design. Lute Suites is a luxury boutique hotel on the edge of the city of Amsterdam. The wallpaper includes enough flourishes and damask patterns to make a minimalist rub his eyes in shock. Oversized ornamentation attracts attention and lets old favorites shine anew.

Lute Suites

Die Niederlande sind bekannt als Quelle spannender Designprodukte. Marcel Wanders ist einer der bekanntesten Designer dieser Herkunft. Aufsehen erregend waren stets seine Möbelentwürfe, sein Blick geht jedoch immer wieder über das singuläre Designobjekt hinaus, hin zu umfassenden Interieurdesign-Konzepten. Die Lute Suites etwa, ein individuell gestaltetes Luxushotel der besonderen Art am Stadtrand von Amsterdam. Angesichts der verwendeten Arabesken, Schnörkeln und Damastmustern reibt sich so mancher Minimalist erstaunt die Augen. Ornamente im Kingsize-Format sorgen für Aufmerksamkeit und lassen Altbekanntes neu erstrahlen.

Lute Suites

La renommée des Pays-Bas dans le domaine du design n'est plus à faire. Marcel Wanders est un des designers les plus connus de la branche. Le mobilier qu'il crée est toujours très remarqué. Mais, loin de s'arrêter au design d'objets, son travail englobe également l'architecture d'intérieur. Les Lute Suites par exemple sont une de ses réalisations. Cet hôtel de luxe, à l'aménagement très individuel, est situé dans un faubourg d'Amsterdam. Plus d'un minimaliste se frottera les yeux de surprise en découvrant la profusion d'arabesques, de fioritures et de motifs de damas. L'élément insolite réside dans le grand format des ornements qui donne à des motifs classiques une certaine modernité.

Every suite has the character of a private house where the guest discovers new design combinations, perhaps getting the urge to have something similar within his or her own four walls at home. It doesn't have to just be the furniture that inspires—maybe it is the bathroom decor, curtain material, or wallpaper that the guests like.

Jedes der Apartments hat den Charakter eines Privathauses. Hier entdecken die Gäste neue Design-Kombinationen und bekommen den Wunsch, Ähnliches auch in den eigenen vier Wänden zu verwirklichen. Das müssen nicht unbedingt nur Möbel sein, auch die verwendeten Werkstoffe im Bad, Gardinenstoffe oder Tapeten inspirieren die Gäste.

Chacune des suites possède le charme et le caractère d'une demeure. Les clients découvrent de nouvelles formes de design qu'ils ont envie ensuite de reproduire. Les meubles ne donnent pas seulement de nouvelles idées de décoration, mais les matières utilisées dans les salles de bains, les tissus des rideaux et les papiers peints inspirent également les hôtes.

Verzeichnis | Index

Directory

5.5 Designers
Paris, France
www.cinqcinqdesigners.com
www.domestic.fr
Photos: Thomas Mailaender

A better tomorrow
Düsseldorf, Germany
www.a-better-tomorrow.com
Photos: Tim Lindemann, Simon Burko

Absolute Zero°
London, United Kingdom
www.absolutezerodegrees.com
Photos: Ian Rippington,
Keith Stephenson, Jon Warren

Birgit Amadori
Frankfurt, Germany
www.amadori.org
Photos courtesy of Birgit Amadori

A.S. Création Tapeten AG
Gummersbach, Germany
www.as-creation.de
Photos courtesy of
A.S. Création Tapeten

AtelierGrün / Olivier Arcioli,
Sandra Hagedorn
Düsseldorf, Germany
www.ateliergruen.de
Photos: Sandra Hagedorn

B+N industries
Burlingame, USA
www.bnind.com
Photos courtesy of B+N industries

bernjus.gisbertz atelier
Frankfurt, Germany
www.bauer-bernjus.de
Photos courtesy of 25hours Hotel

Luigi Colani
Karlsruhe, Germany
www.colani.de
www.marburg.com
Photos courtesy of
Marburger Tapetenfabrik

Dominic Crinson
c/o RFK Architects / Digitile Ltd
London, United Kingdom
www.digitile.co.uk
Photos: Rebecca Pike, Eric Miller

Designkooperation
Copenhagen, Denmark
www.hotelfox.dk
Photos: Volkswagen AG

Deuce Design
Surry Hills, Australia
www.deucedesign.com.au
Photos courtesy of Deuce Design

DrNice
Berlin, Germany
www.drnice.net
Photos courtesy of DrNice,
André Kazenwadel

endless wallpaper
Wuppertal, Germany
www.endless-wallpaper.de
Photos: Andreas Durst

Front Design
Stockholm, Sweden
www.frontdesign.se
Photos: Katja Kristoferson,
Anna Lönnerstam

gohome
Cologne, Germany
www.tapetenagentur.de
Photos: Carsten Malz, TapetenAgentur

ippolito fleitz group
with id_buero
Stuttgart, Germany
www.ifgroup.org
www.i-dbuero.de
Photos: Zooey Braun

jazzunique
Frankfurt, Germany
www.jazzunique.de
Photos courtesy of jazzunique